**W9-BMY-361**

COMPACT *Research*

Conflict in the Middle East

by Clay Farris Naff

Current Issues

ReferencePoint Press™

San Diego, CA

For more information, contact:
ReferencePoint Press, Inc.
PO Box 27779
San Diego, CA 92198
www. ReferencePointPress.com

Picture credits:
Maury Aaseng, 32–35, 49–52, 69–72, 87–90
AP/Wide World Photos, 9, 15

Series design:
Tamia Dowlatabadi

LIBRARY OF CONGRESS CATALOGING-IN-PUBLICATION DATA

Naff, Clay Farris.
  Conflict in the Middle East / by Clay Farris Naff.
    p. cm. — (Compact research)
  Includes bibliographical references and index.
  ISBN-13: 978-1-60152-016-6 (hardback)
  ISBN-10: 1-60152-016-6 (hardback)
  1. Middle East—Politics and government—20th century. 2. Middle East—Politics and government—21st century. 3. Arab-Israeli conflict. I. Title.
  DS62.4.N27 2008
  956.04—dc22
                                                                        2007011617

Contents

Foreword

66 **Where is the knowledge we have lost in information?** 99

—"The Rock," T.S. Eliot.

As modern civilization continues to evolve, its ability to create, store, distribute, and access information expands exponentially. The explosion of information from all media continues to increase at a phenomenal rate. By 2020 some experts predict the worldwide information base will double every 73 days. While access to diverse sources of information and perspectives is paramount to any democratic society, information alone cannot help people gain knowledge and understanding. Information must be organized and presented clearly and succinctly in order to be understood. The challenge in the digital age becomes not the creation of information, but how best to sort, organize, enhance, and present information.

ReferencePoint Press developed the *Compact Research* series with this challenge of the information age in mind. More than any other subject area today, researching current events can yield vast, diverse, and unqualified information that can be intimidating and overwhelming for even the most advanced and motivated researcher. The *Compact Research* series offers a compact, relevant, intelligent, and conveniently organized collection of information covering a variety of current and controversial topics ranging from illegal immigration to marijuana.

The series focuses on three types of information: objective single-author narratives, opinion-based primary source quotations, and facts and statistics. The clearly written objective narratives provide context and reliable background information. Primary source quotes are carefully selected and cited, exposing the reader to differing points of view. And facts and statistics sections aid the reader in evaluating perspectives. Presenting these key types of information creates a richer, more balanced learning experience.

For better understanding and convenience, the series enhances information by organizing it into narrower topics and adding design features that make it easy for a reader to identify desired content. For example, in *Compact Research: Illegal Immigration*, a chapter covering the economic impact of illegal immigration has an objective narrative explaining the various ways the economy is impacted, a balanced section of numerous primary source quotes on the topic, followed by facts and full-color illustrations to encourage evaluation of contrasting perspectives.

The ancient Roman philosopher Lucius Annaeus Seneca wrote, "It is quality rather than quantity that matters." More than just a collection of content, the *Compact Research* series is simply committed to creating, finding, organizing, and presenting the most relevant and appropriate amount of information on a current topic in a user-friendly style that invites, intrigues, and fosters understanding.

Middle East Conflicts at a Glance

Geography

The Middle East is a region that stretches from the middle of North Africa around the eastern shore of the Mediterranean and up into Central Asia.

Population

With a regional population of more than 300 million, the Middle East is home to about 5 percent of the world's people.

Religions

Three major world religions have their roots in the Middle East: Judaism, Christianity, and Islam. A number of minor faiths, such as Baha'i, are also based in the region.

Distribution of Religions

About 85 percent of the region's population in the Middle East are Muslims. Christians make up about 3 percent of the region, and Jews about 2 percent. The rest belong to minor faiths or no faith.

Politics

Most of the countries of the Middle East have dictatorial governments, though some are partial democracies. Israel is generally considered the only state in the region with a stable democracy.

Economies

The Middle East includes some of the richest and poorest countries in the world. Saudi Arabia and other oil-producing countries are wealthy, while Afghanistan is extremely poor.

Resources

About two-thirds of the world's proven oil reserves are located in the Middle East. Petroleum products account for more than 80 percent of the region's income.

Scarcity

The Middle East has less than 1 percent of the world's supply of fresh water. Scarcity of water is becoming a serious problem as populations grow.

Technology

As measured by Internet use, Israel is the only high-tech country in the region. About 75 percent of Israelis use the Internet, compared with 10 percent of Arabs.

Military

Owing to ongoing conflicts, the Middle East is one of the most heavily militarized regions in the world. Both Russia and America sell more arms to the Middle East than anywhere else.

Overview

66 Death is better than living on this Earth with the un-
believers amongst us, making a mockery of our religion and prophet.99

—Al Qaeda Founder Osama bin Laden, 2006.

66 Victory in Iraq will bring something new in the Arab
world—a functioning democracy that polices its territory, upholds the rule of law, respects fundamental
human liberties, and answers to its people.99

—President George W. Bush, 2007.

Virtually everything about the Middle East is contested. Its history, its geography, its politics, even its name—seemingly nothing in the region is above controversy. All the same, everyone can agree upon at least three basic facts.

The Middle East is the cradle of three of the world's most influential religions: Judaism, Christianity, and Islam. As such, the land at the heart of the region holds powerful emotional sway over billions of people.

The Middle East holds the greatest quantities of the world's oil. Since oil fuels the modern economy, the region is critical to the rest of the world.

The Middle East is a region of constant conflict, ranging from civil insurrection to open warfare. For the last half century, many of the world's most powerful nations, especially the United States, have been deeply involved in those conflicts.

In 1979 the Soviet Union invaded Afghanistan. The Soviets faced a determined guerrilla Islamic army, which received clandestine support from the United States and Saudi Arabia. This Afghan guerrilla is using a U.S. made Stinger anti-aircraft missile.

What Is the Middle East?

Controversies over the political geography of the region abound. Some define the Middle East to include everything from Morocco on the western shore of North Africa to Pakistan's border with China. The narrowest definitions exclude Egypt. Some Arab countries argue that "Middle East" should be called "West Asia." The label "Middle East" was first adopted by European leaders early in the twentieth century, a time when the colonial powers of the West were making incursions into what had been a largely unified Islamic empire. As such, the term "Middle East" implies a region viewed from the perspective of its conqueror, which local residents find objectionable. Consequently, the United Nations eschews the term, preferring "Southwest Asia." However, the United States continues to use "Middle East."

The traditional Middle East includes the predominately Arab nations plus the Jewish state of Israel and Iran, which is not Arab but Persian. Some international bodies, including the influential Group of Eight major industrial nations, recognize a "greater Middle East," encompassing most of the Islamic world from the western shores of North Africa to Pakistan's eastern border with China. For purposes of this book the Middle East is defined by common usage and recent political history. It is bounded by Libya on the west, Syria and Iraq to the north, Afghanistan to the east, and Yemen to the south. Among the other key states within those boundaries are Israel, Iran, and Saudi Arabia.

Mists of History

The ancient Middle East was home to numerous peoples. Some, such as the Egyptians, Canaanites, and Babylonians, are found in the Bible (as well as other written records and artifacts). The ancient civilization destined to be most influential in the modern world was that of the Hebrews. Traditionally thought to have been founded by the patriarch Abraham around 1950 B.C., the Hebrews, or Israelites, comprised one people who sometimes lived under a king and sometimes fractured into a coalition of tribes (traditionally reckoned at 12). A literate people, they recorded their struggles to defend themselves against hostile neighbors, their conquests, and the laws they lived by. Some of those records make up portions of the Old Testament. Around 580 B.C. the Babylonians, from what is now Iraq, invaded and enslaved the Israelites. They were later freed by the Persians (from what is now Iran), but slavery and freedom remained important themes in their literature. Throughout their tumultuous history they clung to the monotheistic religion that remains as Judaism today but which along the way gave inspiration to both Christianity and Islam. Indeed, the three faiths together are known to scholars as the Abrahamic religions.

> " The ancient civilization destined to be most influential in the modern world was that of the Hebrews. "

Dawn of Islam

Islam also calls the Middle East home. Early in the seventh century, Muslims believe, the angel Gabriel began to visit the prophet Muhammad with a revelation from Allah (which means "God" in Arabic). Those revelations form the Koran (sometimes rendered as "Qur'an"), the holy scripture of Islam. Muhammad preached the teachings of the Koran in and around Mecca and Medina in what is today Saudi Arabia. His following rapidly grew, and by the time of his death in 632 Islam had become the dominant religion throughout the Arabian Peninsula. A quarrel over the successors to Muhammad led to a schism, with the majority calling themselves Sunni and a minority, now based principally in Iran and Iraq, calling themselves Shia.

> Islam accorded Christians and Jews legal status as members of tolerated faiths.

Despite this split Islam grew rapidly. A century later the predominance of Islam extended across North Africa, up into Spain on its western flank, and east as far as India. Christians and Jews continued to live in the Middle East but were now island communities within an ocean of Islam. In contrast to the treatment of minority religions in other places at the time, Islam accorded Christians and Jews legal status as members of tolerated faiths, called *dhimmis*. However, the success of Islam destined it for conflict with Christian Europe, a conflict that in modern times would evolve into clashes between militant Islam and the secular West.

The first of these clashes was an invasion of the Middle East by European armies. They were dispatched by Pope Urban II in 1095 to wrest Jerusalem and the rest of the Holy Lands away from Islam. The Crusades, as the war between Christendom and Islam became known, continued sporadically for 200 years. It failed to achieve its objective. Many centuries later some people regard Middle Eastern conflicts today as an extension of the Crusades. President George W. Bush has spoken of a "crusade" against Islamic terrorism. Muslim extremists throughout the Middle East see themselves as struggling to repel Western "crusaders" from the Islamic empire through jihad, or holy war.

Ottoman Empire

Beginning in 1300 the Islamic Empire came to be dominated by the Ottomans, a tribe based in Turkey. They ruled and extended their Islamic empire for more than five centuries. At its height in the sixteenth century the Ottoman Empire reached well into Europe, encompassing Constantinople (now Istanbul), Hungary, and the Balkans. Twice, the Ottomans laid siege to Vienna. However, as Western naval prowess grew and colonial riches flowed into Europe, the tide eventually turned. In succeeding centuries internal political decay sealed the fate of the Ottomans. By the late-nineteenth century, their empire had become known as the "sick man of Europe."

World War I destroyed the remnants of Ottoman power. Britain and France, with the backing of the League of Nations, carved the Middle East into dependent states known as "mandates" or "protectorates." Many of these arbitrarily forced incompatible ethnic or religious groups into single nations, sowing the seeds of later civil conflicts. A notable instance is Iraq. Once the seat of the Babylonian Empire, modern Iraq was created by the 1916 Sykes-Picot agreement between Britain and France. This secret deal enabled Britain to take control of Iraq in 1920 in the aftermath of World War I. The boundaries dictated by the European powers divided the non-Arab Kurds among Turkey, Iraq, and Iran. Kurds in northern Iraq rebelled and were brutally repressed by the British. The British also imposed a Sunni kingdom on Iraq, to the dismay of the Shiite majority in the south. This too sowed seeds of a later conflict, which America inherited after its 2003 invasion of Iraq.

Iraq Wars

Violence was by no means confined to the Arab-Israeli conflict. From 1980 until his overthrow in 2003, Iraqi dictator Saddam Hussein played an exceptionally belligerent role in the Middle East. Following a 1979 revolution in Iran, Saddam launched an eight-year war against his neighbor to the east. Four years after an uneasy peace with Iran, he invaded neighboring Kuwait to the south and seized its oil fields. That invasion was turned back by a U.S.-led coalition in 1991, during what has come to be known as Operation Desert Storm. In 2003 President George W. Bush, son of the president who directed Desert Storm, led a much smaller coalition of forces in an invasion of Iraq that overthrew Saddam's regime. U.S. forces and a dwindling number of partners have faced an increasingly violent insurrection ever since. Many argue that the insurrection has devolved into civil war between two sects of Muslims—the Sunnis, who held power under Saddam, and the Shiites, who form the majority of Iraqis.

Al Qaeda and 9/11

At the fringe of the Middle East, the 1979 Soviet invasion of Afghanistan initiated a series of events that culminated in the most significant terrorist attack in history. The Soviets were attempting to prop up a Communist president. However, they were opposed by a guerrilla Islamic army, which received clandestine support from the United States and Saudi Arabia. One Saudi who became directly involved in the fight against the Soviet invaders was Osama bin Laden. Using his family fortune, he founded an underground resistance organization in Afghanistan. It later became the notorious terrorist group "al Qaeda," Arabic for "the base." Following the withdrawal of the Soviets and the installation of a radical Islamic regime called the Taliban, al Qaeda focused on driving Americans out of the Middle East and, more nebulously, restoring the Islamic empire. It organized a series of terrorist attacks against U.S. targets, including embassies in East Africa and the U.S. naval vessel *Cole*. In September 2001 al Qaeda launched spectacular and deadly attacks on the U.S. homeland in what came to be known as 9/11. On that

> " Using his family fortune, Bin Laden founded an underground resistance organization in Afghanistan. It later became the notorious terrorist group 'al Qaeda,' Arabic for 'the base.' "

day, using hijacked airliners, al Qaeda operatives brought down the Twin Towers in New York City, severely damaged the Pentagon, and crashed another plane into a field in Pennsylvania.

In response the United States invaded Afghanistan late in 2001 and overthrew the Taliban. It later invaded Iraq, which the Bush administration claimed was in league with al Qaeda and was preparing weapons of mass destruction. Both claims later proved unfounded, but in the aftermath of the invasion al Qaeda did set up operations in Iraq and had considerable success in its avowed strategy of inflaming sectarian violence between Sunnis and Shiites so as to make the nation ungovernable.

How Does Militant Religion Fuel Middle East Conflicts?

Religion has always been important in the Middle East, but its role in conflicts has grown tremendously in recent decades. During the Cold War, from the end of World War II until the 1980s, most governments and leading ideologies in the Middle East were mainly secular. The Palestine Liberation Organization (PLO), for example, was a secular organization, and Israel, though explicitly a Jewish state, emphasized its Socialist leanings in the early years. The situation has changed drastically in recent decades. Iran, for decades under the control of the West-supported shah, underwent an Islamic revolution that left it violently opposed to the United States. In Israel militant believers pressed for a "Greater Israel," conforming to what they believe were the biblical frontiers of the Jewish nation. In the Arab states militant Islamist movements emerged as terrorist threats. And among the Palestinians, following the death of longtime leader Yasir Arafat in 2004, the Islamist Hamas organization wrested control away from the PLO. The Iranian-backed Hizballah ("Party of God") has become one of the most powerful actors in Lebanon.

> " In Israel militant believers pressed for a 'Greater Israel,' conforming to what they believe were the biblical frontiers of the Jewish nation. "

The effect of militant religion in the Middle East has been profoundly negative. Religious extremists have consistently undermined attempts to make peace. Peacemakers have been frequent targets of assassination. Among the most notable to die were Egyptian president Anwar Sadat and Israeli prime minister Yitzhak Rabin. Each was killed by fellow citizens whose zealotry rendered peace an unbearable prospect. Fanatics on all sides have engaged in the slaugh-

The Israeli army, positioned along the Lebanese border, fires shells at Lebanon's Hizballah guerrillas during a 2004 exchange at a disputed area. The Iranian-backed Hizballah has become one of the most powerful players in Lebanon.

ter of innocent civilians, most recently on a daily basis in Iraq. Shoppers, worshippers, and schoolchildren have all been among their targets.

What Is the U.S. Role in the Middle East?

Since the end of World War II the United States has tried to play a dual role in the Middle East. On the one hand it has been the leading sponsor and ally of Israel. President Harry Truman led the postwar effort to gain acceptance for a partition of Palestine (then under British control) into Jewish and Arab states. Under Truman the United States became the first country to recognize Israel after it declared independence on May 14, 1948. In the decades since, U.S. financial and military aid have been key to Israel's survival against hostile neighbors.

On the other hand, the United States has tried to befriend key Arab states to play the role of honest broker for peace so as to assure access to oil supplies. The conflicting roles came into sharp relief during the 1973 "Yom Kippur" war between Arab states and Israel, when the oil-producing nations of the Middle East reduced sales to the West in protest of the U.S. role as chief supporter of Israel. Shortages of oil caused long lines at gas stations and major economic disruptions.

> **Both [Iraq and Afghanistan] have indeed held democratic elections. However, both countries are experiencing violent insurrection and enormous economic and political chaos.**

The peacemaker role reached its apogee in the 1978 Camp David accords, when President Jimmy Carter brought Sadat and Israeli premier Menachem Begin together to work out a peace treaty that has survived to the present day. Bush radically altered the U.S. approach to peace in the Middle East with the 2001 invasion of Afghanistan and the 2003 invasion of Iraq, which he has subsequently said is intended to create a model of democracy for the Arab world. Both nations have indeed held democratic elections. However, both countries are experiencing violent insurrection and enormous economic and political chaos. Few observers believe that other Middle Eastern countries will voluntarily follow their example.

The U.S. role in the Middle East has come under intensifying criticism since the 2003 invasion of Iraq. With the exception of a few allies such as Britain, the major powers of the world opposed the invasion. Numerous countries have since accused the United States of invading Iraq on false pretenses and of having done an inadequate job of protecting civilians and rebuilding its economy in the years since. Meantime, criticism has grown over the Bush administration's policies regarding the Israeli-Palestinian conflict. In particular, critics have lamented the lack of resumption of peace talks of any kind between the Palestinians and Israelis since 2000. Furthermore, in Afghanistan, the one place where there was little outside opposition to U.S. intervention, concerns have grown that the Taliban may be making a comeback.

Palestinian-Israeli Conflict

Perhaps the most significant development in the modern history of the Middle East was the founding of the state of Israel. With its creation in 1948 by a United Nations resolution, Jews who had suffered genocide in Nazi-dominated Europe rejoiced, but Arabs felt betrayed. Feeling the West had promised them sovereignty over their lands, they united in opposition to the Jewish state, and war immediately followed. Israel, backed by the United States, won and continued to win periodic regional wars against the combined forces of the Arab states. During the Six Day War of 1967, a victorious Israel seized additional territory including the Sinai from Egypt, the West Bank and Gaza from Jordan, and the Golan Heights from Syria. These became the basis of continuing dispute, which flared again into war in 1973. Only Egypt has so far recovered substantial territory, which Israel returned in exchange for a peace treaty in 1978. The crux of the Arab-Israeli conflict, however, has been the displacement of the Palestinian people. During the 1948–1949 War of Independence, a large number of Arabs living in what is now Israel fled or were driven from their homes. They and their offspring have lived in exile ever since. Their frustration has led to violent, often terroristic, attacks on Israelis and Westerners. Attempts to broker a two-state solution—Israel and Palestine—have foundered, and mutual violence continues.

Is Peace Possible in the Middle East?

In the face of so many unyielding conflicts, some are questioning whether a comprehensive and lasting peace can be achieved in the Middle East. There are some who believe that only the application of maximum military force can create conditions under which peace will become possible. There are others who believe that only diplomatic efforts will yield peace.

> **Everyone agrees that nowhere in the world is peace more difficult to achieve than in the Middle East.**

Everyone agrees that nowhere in the world is peace more difficult to achieve than in the Middle East. Every habitable acre of the region has been violently contested for generations, leaving the present-day inhabitants with deep-seated grievances and a disinclination to trust anyone outside their own clan, tribe, or coreligionists. Moreover, the increasing reliance on religion to justify claims and actions makes compromise seemingly impossible. When people believe they are acting on behalf of God's will, concession becomes blasphemous.

A growing number in Israel believe that they can achieve peace for themselves through unilateral actions. These include building barriers between themselves and the Palestinians in Gaza and the West Bank and then declaring a two-state solution. The Palestinians strongly object to this approach. They argue that Israel is building its wall through territory that is traditionally and legally the property of Palestinians. Moreover, they argue that a Palestinian state divided into two sections separated by Israel cannot be viable. Such a peace, imposed against the will of one party, will demand considerable military force to maintain. To some observers, this is no peace at all; to others, it is the best option available to Israel.

In the view of some key leaders and analysts, including the congressionally appointed Iraq Study Group and former president Jimmy Carter, comprehensive and just peace, though immensely difficult, is possible. In this view, negotiation among all the interested parties is the key, along with a willingness of outsiders such as the United States to invest in peace. In support of this view, they point to progress already achieved. The 1978 Camp David Accords brought lasting peace between Egypt and Israel. Jordan has also made peace with Israel. The Oslo Accords showed that Israelis and Palestinians could sit down together and sign peace agreements. In subsequent negotiations they came very close to making total peace, and the fact that they fell short does not mean that future attempts at peace will fail. Of course, that is not the only Mideast situation where peace is needed.

Iraq

Iraq has been in constant turmoil since the 2003 U.S. invasion. Despite the nightmarish conditions of strife in Iraq, optimists hold that bringing all the surrounding countries into negotiations with the Iraqis themselves could help to stabilize Iraq's fragile democracy and bring a measure of peace to that troubled land.

Afghanistan's troubled republic may yet hold. A European-led force has promised to bolster its democratically elected government against the resurgent forces of the Taliban.

A Time of Reckoning

Even the most optimistic observer must concede that the outlook for the region is cloudy. Few places on Earth have more uncertain prospects for peace than the Middle East, and nowhere are the stakes higher.

Among the looming threats to peace are terrorism, civil war, and nuclear weapons. Israel is known to have nuclear weapons, and Iran is apparently on the way to acquiring them. Saudi Arabia, feeling threatened by Iran, has declared its intention to seek a nuclear weapon as well. Clashes between Israel and its opponents continue to flare. New conflicts are brewing—Sunnis and Shiites are opposed in what some term a civil war in Iraq, and the Palestinians are driven by armed conflict between the Islamist Hamas faction and the more secular Fatah faction.

Furthermore, petroleum, the single most important resource in the global economy, is dwindling. New discoveries are rare; old wells are running dry. Iraq, Iran, Saudi Arabia, and a few other Middle Eastern states hold the lion's share of remaining oil. Experts say shortages and rising prices are likely within a decade.

These developments do not rule out the possibility of peace, but they do present a likely limit on the time available for its realization. By the same token, tranquility in the Middle East is in the interest of the entire world, and most especially the hundreds of millions of inhabitants of that blood-soaked region. With the trend lines pointing to a crisis, the search for peace cannot be put off for long.

How Has the Rise of Islamic Militancy Affected Middle East Conflicts?

66 [Al Qaeda] is the terrorist organization that poses the greatest threat to US interests, including to the Homeland. . . . They continue to plot attacks against our Homeland and other targets with the objective of inflicting mass casualties. 99

—John D. Negroponte, U.S. Director of National Intelligence.

66 Amid this unjust war, the war of infidels and debauchees led by America along with its allies and agents, we would like to stress: . . . God Almighty says: 'Those who believe fight in the cause of Allah, and those who reject faith fight in the cause of evil.' So fight ye against the friends of Satan. 99

—Osama bin Laden, founder of the Islamist terrorist organization al Qaeda.

Islam, like other major faiths, encompasses a wide variety of beliefs and practices. Many, including President George W. Bush, have called it a religion of peace. At times in its history, Islam has had periods of both expansive violence and peaceful stability. In recent decades, however, a radical new tendency toward global violent extremism has emerged from within Islam. There is no single organization or ideology behind this militancy, but characteristically nonstate actors are involved, ranging from underground terrorist groups to political parties to religious welfare organizations. The ideology that animates the militancy is a highly aggressive interpretation of Islam that envisions a global jihad (holy war) against what they term "the infidels." This violent movement has been termed "Islamism."

Islamism is not endorsed by all Muslims. In fact, relatively few of the world's more than 1 billion Muslims are involved in any kind of organized violence. Moreover, whereas mainstream Islam draws its principles from the ancient text of the Koran and the sayings of the prophet Muhammad, Islamism takes much of its direction from the twentieth-century writings of Egyptian intellectual Sayid Qutb and other anti-Western Muslim activists. Despite its marginal status, however, Islamic militancy has become a highly significant factor in international relations.

The Global Threat of al Qaeda

The Islamist group that has attracted the most worldwide attention is al Qaeda. Directly or indirectly it has claimed responsibility for some of the most heinous terrorist acts of recent times. Its hallmark is the suicide attack. Al Qaeda did not originate the suicide attack, but it has put it to the most dramatic uses, in attacks ranging from the Twin Towers of New York City to commuter trains in Spain to the conflict in Iraq.

Al Qaeda was born on the fringes of the Middle East, out of ashes of the 1979 Soviet invasion of Afghanistan. The Soviets were opposed by a guerrilla Islamic army composed of volunteers from all over the Middle East, which received clandestine support from the United States and Saudi Arabia. Among the Saudis who became directly involved in the fight against the Soviet invaders was Osama bin Laden. Using his family fortune, he founded an underground resistance organization in Afghanistan which came to be called "al Qaeda," Arabic for "the base."

> **Relatively few of the world's more than 1 billion Muslims are involved in any kind of organized violence.**

In the 1990s, following the withdrawal of the Soviets and the installation of a radical Islamic regime called the Taliban, al Qaeda focused on driving Americans out of the Middle East and, more nebulously, restoring the Islamic empire. It organized a series of terrorist attacks against

U.S. targets, including embassies in East Africa and the U.S. naval vessel *Cole*. In September 2001 al Qaeda launched spectacular and deadly attacks on the U.S. homeland in what came to be known as 9/11. On that day, using hijacked airliners, al Qaeda operatives brought down the Twin Towers in New York City, crashed into the Pentagon, and crashed another plane into a field in Pennsylvania. The day's death toll came to more than 3,000 people, and led Bush to declare a "War on Terror," with al Qaeda as the principal target.

> " The United States led an invasion of Afghanistan late in 2001 and overthrew the Taliban, but the leaders of al Qaeda escaped. "

The United States led an invasion of Afghanistan late in 2001 and overthrew the Taliban, but the leaders of al Qaeda escaped. U.S. forces have continued to seize al Qaeda suspects and disrupt networks. In 2004 the administration declared that al Qaeda had been seriously damaged. Its leaders remain in hiding, and its centralized structure has been broken up. Its key planner of terrorist operations, Khalid Shaikh Mohammed, has been confined for years at the U.S. base in Guantánamo, and in 2007 he confessed to a long series of attacks.

In the judgment of many analysts, however, al Qaeda has adapted to new conditions and remains a global threat. In its new form, al Qaeda is a horizontal network of independently operating cells that collaborate via the Internet and a shadowy network of couriers and financiers. An example of this new style of operation is the 2002 suicide bombing of a nightclub on the Indonesian resort island of Bali, which killed 180 people and wounded many others. The totally unexpected attack (Bali had been noted for its tranquillity) turned out to be the work of an Indonesian group called Jemaah Islamiya, which proved to be an affiliate of al Qaeda. Other post-9/11 al Qaeda–linked terrorist attacks include a bombing of Madrid's commuter trains in 2004 that left 202 people dead, and suicide bombings in London's commuter system in 2005 that killed more than 50 people. In a sober assessment delivered to Congress on January 11, 2007, U.S. director of national intelligence John D. Negroponte declared that al Qaeda remains the greatest terrorist threat to the United States.

Renewed Islamic Militancy in Afghanistan

Following a 2001 U.S.-led invasion, Afghanistan now has a democratically elected government. However, that government faces severe challenges. The Taliban, an Islamist movement that formerly ruled the country, is making a comeback. Worse yet, the threat to democracy is accompanied by a spectacular rise in the production of heroin. U.S. intelligence agency reports indicate that the Taliban is financing its resurgence by taking a share of drug profits in exchange for providing protection.

U.S. forces routed the Taliban in late 2001 but failed to capture its leaders, who are believed to have escaped into the tribal territories of neighboring Pakistan. There they rebuilt their capacity to strike and adopted new tactics, such as suicide bombing.

According to the journal *Foreign Policy in Focus*, a combination of institutional weakness in the democratically elected government of Afghan president Hamid Karzai and the effectiveness of the Taliban's tactics have left the country in chaos. Outside the capital of Kabul, warlords, many of whom are thought to collaborate with the Taliban, predominate. Many of Afghanistan's inhabitants are worse off economically than before the invasion (when international sanctions were in place), and support for the Taliban is growing. Although the Taliban is not regarded as a global actor, its renewed challenge in Afghanistan has pinned down U.S. and European forces that might otherwise be involved in conflicts elsewhere.

> " U.S. intelligence agency reports indicate that the Taliban is financing its resurgence by taking a share of drug profits. "

Islamic Terrorism in Iraq

Iraq has become a major focus of al Qaeda operations. Unlike in other places, where its operations have been sporadic, al Qaeda has operated nonstop in Iraq since the 2003 U.S.-led invasion. Its strategy of thwarting U.S. postwar goals there has been largely successful. Al Qaeda first drove the United Nations and other nongovernmental aid organizations out of the country with a series of vicious bombings and kidnappings. It then set about inflaming sectarian violence between Iraqi Sunnis and Shiites so as to make the nation ungovernable.

Their task has been made easier by a host of Iraqi terrorist groups on both sides of the sectarian divide. Even so, for years many members of the two major sects of Islam resisted provocations to turn against one another.

However, a turning point came on February 22, 2006, when al Qaeda operatives bombed the al-Askari Mosque in the Iraqi city of Samarra. The famed golden dome of the mosque, one of the holiest sites in Shia Islam, collapsed. Enraged Shiites went on a rampage, and a massacre of Sunnis took place, setting off cycles of revenge killings. These have continued to escalate to the point that even the U.S. military has reluctantly begun to describe the situation in Iraq as a civil war.

Iran and Hizballah

Since an Islamic revolution overthrew the American-backed shah in 1979, Iran has been deeply involved in Middle East conflicts. Iran differs from most Middle Eastern nations. It is non-Arab (its people are the descendants of Persians), and it is the only major country with an officially Shiite government. The highly conservative religious leadership of Iran has frequently proclaimed "Death to America," which it sometimes refers to as "the Great Satan." An eight-year war with Iraq in the 1980s left it somewhat weakened, but in recent years, with Iraq in chaos and oil prices near record highs, Iran has begun to assert itself again on many fronts.

> "The highly conservative religious leadership of Iran has frequently proclaimed 'Death to America.'"

In Iraq, according to the Bush administration, Iranian Revolutionary Guards have been supplying armor-piercing weapons to Shiite radicals for use against U.S. forces. Iran denies the charges, but no one doubts that Iran exerts great influence over powerful Shiite militias under the command of radical cleric Moqtada al-Sadr. It is those militias that have frequently clashed with U.S. and British forces in Iraq.

Iran has also turned its sights on Israel. In 2005 Iranian president Mahmoud Ahmadinejad declared that Israel should be wiped off the map. The remark brought widespread condemnation. Defiantly, Ahmadinejad followed up those remarks by organizing a conference of Holocaust deniers in the Iranian capital of Tehran. The conference brought international condemnation, even from some Muslim commentators. Although Holocaust denial is commonplace in the Arab world, distrust of Iran's motives runs high. Saudi journalist Yousef Al-Sweidan excoriated Ahmadinejad's grandstanding. "The new extremist Nazis in turbans were not ashamed to open that wretched conference," he wrote, "spreading hate and tendentious propaganda and defending the heinous crimes of the Nazis."[1]

International condemnation has not restrained Iran, however. Indeed, it has gone well beyond words in its hostility toward Israel and the West. Iran has long been the chief sponsor of Hizballah, or "Party of God," a militant Shiite organization in Lebanon. In the summer of 2006 Hizballah launched a barrage of rockets against Israel. For the first time, these included longer range rockets with the capability of striking Israeli urban centers. Israel reacted with a monthlong bombing campaign throughout Lebanon. Eventually, a truce was reached. Although Iran has not been conclusively proven to be responsible, Israel accuses Iran of directly supporting the attacks with money and arms.

In March 2007 Iran again raised international concern when it seized 15 British naval personnel who, Britain maintained, were operating in Iraqi waters. Before releasing them the Iranians forced the prisoners to make public confessions and apologies on television. The incident sent oil prices climbing and led the U.S. Navy to deploy additional aircraft carriers in the waters off Iran.

Iran's Nuclear Program

Of greatest concern to the international community is Iran's nuclear development program. The United States and other countries accuse Iran of working to develop nuclear weapons. Iran denies this, claiming that its nuclear program is intended for electrical generation only. However, the Islamic state has been defiant in the face of international demands that it stop enriching uranium and subject its program to international safeguards aimed at insuring that nuclear power does not lead to nuclear weapons. In December 2006 the United Nations Security Council unanimously passed a resolution imposing a global ban on the shipment of nuclear materials to Iran and imposing limited economic sanctions. In April

2007 Iran again showed defiance. On April 9 Ahmadinejad declared that his country was now able to produce nuclear fuel on an "industrial scale," which aides said meant that Iran will install as many as 50,000 centrifuges to ramp up its ability to enrich uranium.

This hard-line stance has led many in the West to suspect that Iran is determined to develop nuclear weapons. This raises deep fears, because Israel is known to have a nuclear weapons arsenal. As far back as 2001 Ayatollah Ali Akbar Hashemi-Rafsanjani, one of Iran's senior clerics and a former president of the nation, declared that Iran could survive a nuclear exchange with Israel, while Israel would be obliterated.

> "Iran's hard-line stance has led many in the West to suspect that Iran is determined to develop nuclear weapons."

Western nations and Israel have reacted with alarm and consternation to Iran's nuclear ambitions. The European Union "views Iran's announcement that it wants to enrich uranium on an industrial scale with great concern,"[2] according to a statement from its president. The White House also expressed concern about the announcement and called on Iran to comply with United Nations resolutions. However, there appears to be little that the international community can do to force Iran to cooperate. The world needs the oil that Iran sells, and military analysts say that Iran has distributed and protected its nuclear program too well to be vulnerable to attack.

Complicating matters, Saudi Arabia has reportedly begun seeking nuclear capability for itself. The world's largest oil producer, Saudi Arabia is a staunchly Sunni Muslim country that is wary of Shiite Iran. Should either one obtain nuclear weapons, a catastrophic conflict could ensue. Israel is known to have an arsenal of at least 100 nuclear weapons. The compact geography of the Middle East, combined with the deep hatred and mistrust, could raise the probability of an accidental, let alone an intentional, nuclear war. Hundreds of millions of lives would be in jeopardy, and the world's economy would face a crippling blow due to the disruption of oil production in the Middle East.

How Has the Rise of Islamic Militancy Affected Middle East Conflicts?

❝You provide the jihad with a technology that will defeat the crusaders' modern technology. Your bodies are our new cruise missiles and atom bombs.❞

—Mullah Dadullah Ahkund, quoted in Sami Yousafzai and Ron Moreau, "Suicide Offensive," *Newsweek*, April 6, 2007.

Ahkund, a commander of the Taliban's insurgent forces, spoke to recruits in spring 2007 while preparing for a summer offensive. He was killed in fighting a few weeks later.

❝In nearly all cases, the jihadi terrorists have a patently self-evident ambition: to establish a world dominated by Muslims, Islam, and Islamic law.❞

—Daniel Pipes, "What Do the Terrorists Want?" *New York Sun*, July 26, 2005. www.danielpipes.org.

Pipes is a historian and national security analyst. He is founder of the Middle East Forum.

---

* Editor's Note: While the definition of a primary source can be narrowly or broadly defined, for the purposes of Compact Research, a primary source consists of: 1) results of original research presented by an organization or researcher; 2) eyewitness accounts of events, personal experience, or work experience; 3) first-person editorials offering pundits' opinions; 4) government officials presenting political plans and/or policies; 5) representatives of organizations presenting testimony or policy

❝The Koran includes passages invoking violence. But so does the Old Testament, in considerable number.❞

—Antony T. Sullivan, "Should Policymakers See Islam as an Enemy of the West?" *Insight on the News,* November 5, 2001.

Sullivan is a writer and lecturer specializing in the Middle East.

❝For more than a thousand years, Islam provided the only universally acceptable set of rules and principles for the regulation of public and social life.... In recent years there have been many signs that these notions and attitudes may be returning, albeit in much modified forms, to their previous dominance.❞

—Bernard Lewis, *What Went Wrong? The Clash Between Islam and Modernity in the Middle East.*
New York: HarperCollins, 2003.

Lewis, a historian and presidential adviser, is considered by many to be the United States' leading authority on Islam.

❝Militant Islamists do not hate the West because of Israel, they hate Israel because of the West. They see it as the quintessential representative of the free and, in their eyes, hedonistic and corrupt Western civilization they despise so much.❞

—Ophir Falk, "WW III—Understanding and Confronting the Threat," Institute for Counter Terrorism,
January 18, 2007. www.ict.org.il.

Falk is a research fellow at the Institute for Counter Terrorism in Israel and a partner at the Naveh Kantor Even-Har Law Firm.

66 One of the myths that clutters this table is the insistence—mostly by know-nothing American Zionists—that the roots of this conflict are religious. Palestinians (it is claimed) attack Israel because they hate Jews. . . . But it is—start to finish—a lie. In the first place, Islam does not teach hate for Jews, but accords its deepest respect (deepest among non-Muslims) to . . . Christians and Jews. 99

—Richard Ben Cramer, *How Israel Lost: The Four Questions.* New York: Simon and Schuster, 2004.

Cramer has won a Pulitzer prize for his reporting on the Middle East.

66 The establishment of the Zionist regime was a move by the world oppressor against the Islamic world. . . . As the Imam said, Israel must be wiped off the map. 99

—Mahmoud Ahmadinejad, quoted in Al Jazeera, "Ahmadinejad: Wipe Israel off Map," October 28, 2005. http://english.aljazeera.net.

Ahmadinejad was elected president of Iran in August 2005.

66 Iran is the main benefactor of the Hizbullah. It provides funding, weapons and directives for this terrorist organization. 99

—Gideon Meir, "Statement on Hizbullah," July 13, 2006. www.mfa.gov.il.

Meir is the deputy director general of Israel's Foreign Ministry.

❝The effort to negotiate Iran out of its nuclear weapons program has failed and is failing now and needs to be changed dramatically. What we need to do is decisively increase the pressure economically and politically on Iran, ultimately leading to regime change.❞

—John Bolton, quoted in *International Herald Tribune,* "Bolton Says Negotiations with Iran on Nuclear Ambitions Have Failed," Associated Press, April 10, 2007. www.iht.com.

Bolton was the U.S. ambassador to the United Nations during the first years of George W. Bush's second-term presidency.

❝If a day comes when the world of Islam is duly equipped with the arms Israel has in possession, the strategy of colonialism would face a stalemate because application of an atomic bomb would not leave anything in Israel but the same thing would just produce damages in the Muslim world.❞

—Ayatollah Ali Akbar Hashemi-Rafsanjani, quoted in Iran Press Service, "Rafsanjani Says Muslims Should Use Nuclear Weapon Against Israel," December 2001. www.iran-press-service.com.

Rafsanjani is a powerful senior cleric in Iran. He was formerly the president of Iran.

How Has the Rise of Islamic Militancy Affected Middle East Conflicts?

- Islam is the second-largest religion in the world. There are about **1.2 billion** Muslims worldwide.

- The Middle East is unique in being the origin of three highly influential world religions and a number of minor ones. **Judaism, Christianity, and Islam** have their origins there.

- Muslims are in the majority in all Middle East countries except Israel. About **85 percent** of the region's inhabitants are Muslim.

- Islam accords special tolerated status to Christianity and Judaism. In recent years, however, **Muslim extremists** have persecuted both groups in Middle East countries.

- Sunni Muslims are the majority sect of Islam, comprising about **85 percent** of the total. Only in Iran, Iraq, and possibly Bahrain are Shiite Muslims the majority.

- In 2005 over **11,000 terrorist** incidents worldwide resulted in more than **14,000 deaths,** according to the U.S. State Department.

- Islamists are responsible for more than **50 percent** of all terrorist attacks, according to the National Counterterrorism Center.

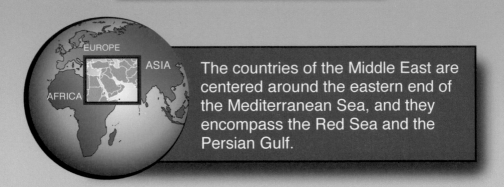

The Modern Middle East

The countries of the Middle East are centered around the eastern end of the Mediterranean Sea, and they encompass the Red Sea and the Persian Gulf.

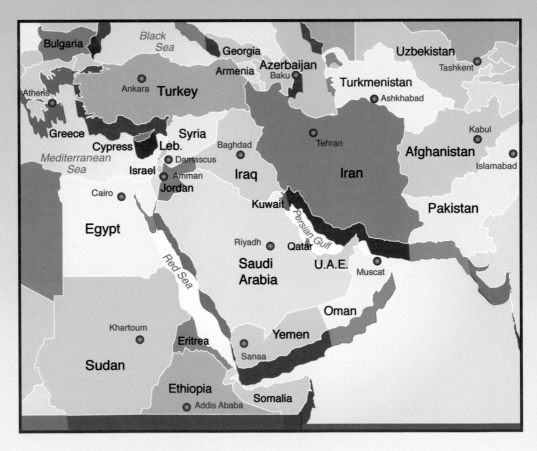

Source: "Historical Maps of Pakistan Region," undated. www.homepagez.com.

Most Muslims Are Against Suicide Bombing

According to a global survey, although some Muslims support suicide bombings, they are widely opposed. Nigeria is an exception. There, nearly 50 percent of Muslims see suicide bombings as sometimes justified.

*Violence against civilian targets in order to defend Islam can be justified...

	Often/ Sometimes	Rarely	Never	Don't Know
France	16%	19%	64%	1%
Spain	16%	9%	69%	7%
Britian	15%	9%	70%	6%
Germany	7%	6%	83%	3%
Jordan	29%	28%	43%	0%
Egypt	28%	25%	45%	3%
Turkey	17%	9%	61%	14%
Pakistan	14%	8%	69%	8%
Indonesia	10%	18%	71%	1%
Nigeria	46%	23%	28%	3%

*asked of Muslims only

Source: Pew Global Attitudes Project, "The Great Divide: How Westerners and Muslims View Each Other," June 12, 2006. http://pewglobal.org.

- The **targets of Islamic radicals** include a number of Arab governments as well as Israelis, Europeans, Americans, and Hindus.

- Sunni-Shiite violence in Iraq has resulted in the deaths of more than **34,000 people,** according to the United Nations.

Distribution of Religions in the Middle East

Muslims are a majority in every Middle East country except Israel, where Jews are in the majority. Christians are a minority in much of the region.

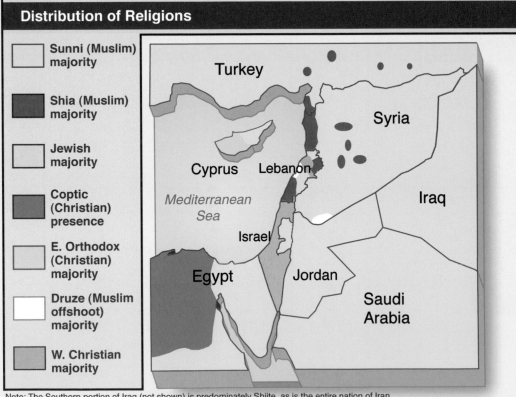

Distribution of Religions

Sunni (Muslim) majority

Shia (Muslim) majority

Jewish majority

Coptic (Christian) presence

E. Orthodox (Christian) majority

Druze (Muslim offshoot) majority

W. Christian majority

Turkey

Syria

Cyprus   Lebanon

Mediterranean Sea

Iraq

Israel

Egypt   Jordan

Saudi Arabia

Note: The Southern portion of Iraq (not shown) is predominately Shiite, as is the entire nation of Iran.

Source: Patricia B. McRae, "Government and Politics of the Middle East: Map Page: Distribution of Religions," Muhlenberg College, 2004. http://drmcsclasses.homestead.com.

Most Muslims Live Outside the Mideast Region

The Muslim population is not confined to the Middle East. In fact, there are more Muslims in South Asia, from Pakistan to Indonesia, than there are in the entire Middle East.

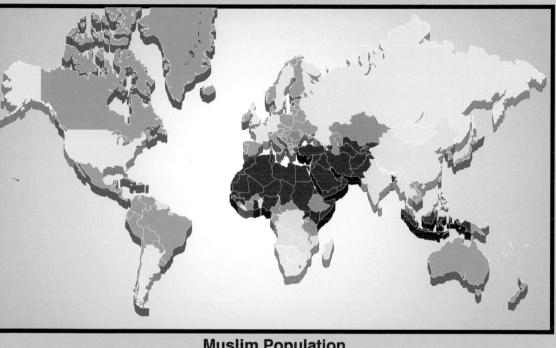

Muslim Population

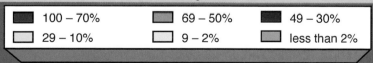

100 – 70%	69 – 50%	49 – 30%
29 – 10%	9 – 2%	less than 2%

Source: Northern Virginia Community College, "Introduction to Islam," 2006. www.nvcc.edu.

- More than **50 known radical Islamist groups** exist worldwide. Many of them are linked under the banner—if not the organization—of al Qaeda.

How Does U.S. Involvement Affect the Middle East?

❝Most people want to live in peace in Iraq. There are extremists who can't stand the thought of a free society. . . . A contagion of violence could spill out across the country, and in time the violence could affect the entire region. What happens in the Middle East matters here in America.❞

—George W. Bush, "President Bush Discusses Iraq War Supplemental, War on Terror."

❝Four years after the fall of Baghdad, the war that was supposed to be a 'cakewalk' has disintegrated into a civil war with our brave men and women in uniform stuck in the middle. . . . Democrats are standing up for our troops by offering a clear and reasonable plan to get our troops out of the middle of the Iraqi civil war.❞

—Howard Dean, Democratic National Committee Chairman.

America is without question the most influential outside power in the Middle East. By the same token, no region of the world has more impact on the United States' foreign policy than the Middle East.

This has become especially true in the aftermath of the U.S. invasion of Iraq. The March 2003 invasion easily defeated Iraq's army, but the aftermath has proven both an embarrassment and a burden. The embarrassment came when it turned out that Iraq had no weapons of mass destruction and that intelligence linking Iraq to al Qaeda was false. Many, including former intelligence officials, charge that the evidence had been trumped up. However, for supporters of the Bush administration's Iraq policy, the faulty intelligence is now irrelevant. They argue that Iraq has become the central front in the global war on terror and that America must pursue victory there. Meantime, other Middle East conflicts continue to demand U.S. attention.

Commitment to Iraq

Since the invasion of 2003 well over 100,000 U.S. forces have been continuously present in Iraq. Thousands more civilian contractors accompany them. This massive deployment of U.S. personnel has had a powerful effect on perceptions of America in the region, but has had only limited success in achieving the Bush administration's stated objectives in Iraq. Ever since the U.S. military routed the Iraqi army and captured Saddam Hussein, it has faced a deadly guerrilla war. At least three different enemies are battling U.S. forces: local Sunni militants who had enjoyed privilege under the former regime, foreign Sunni militants who are drawn to Iraq by al Qaeda, and Shiite militants who are followers of radical cleric Moqtada al-Sadr. (There are other opponents of the U.S. presence in Iraq, but these are the major groupings.) The insurgents make extensive use of hidden roadside bombs, known in military parlance as Improvised Explosive Devices, or IEDs, and suicide bombers. These attacks have effectively prevented the reconstruction of the country and the implementation of effective democratic government.

> "Insurgents make extensive use of hidden roadside bombs and suicide bombers."

According to numerous analysts, including Richard N. Haas, president of the Council on Foreign Relations, the U.S. invasion of Iraq has weakened U.S. military capability, tarnished world opinion of America, and strengthened the ranks of terrorists. The major regional effects of the invasion were to greatly enhance the power of Iran and to unleash a virulent hatred between Sunni and Shiite Muslims. A significant consequence for the United States has been a loss of reputation throughout the Middle East. According to Egypt's president Hosni Mubarak, in the wake of the Iraq invasion an unprecedented hatred for America now exists throughout the Middle East.

The 2006 National Intelligence Estimate, a classified consensus of the U.S. intelligence agencies, also concludes that the Iraq invasion has boosted Islamic terrorist recruitment, according to portions leaked to the media. The Bush administration contends that, though mistakes were made, the victory in Iraq continues to be the best U.S. option. Congress, led since late 2006 by Democrats, argues for handing over responsibility for security to the Iraqi government and pulling U.S. troops out.

America's Alliance with Israel

The United States was the first country to recognize Israel in 1948, and it has been its closest ally ever since. Military aid began to flow soon after its founding, and over the decades Israel has become the largest recipient by far of American assistance, both military and economic. The *Washington Report on Middle East Affairs* estimates that since its inception Israel has received more than $80 billion in U.S. assistance. In recent years the amount of aid has climbed to more than $2 billion annually.

U.S. support has grown stronger over the years. According to Mitchell Bard, executive director of the American-Israeli Cooperative Enterprise, the relationship "has evolved over the last half century into a web of military, economic, academic, bureaucratic and personal connections"[3] that override policy differences.

> " The deep alliance with Israel has complicated U.S. attempts to foster peace with the Palestinians. "

That deep alliance with Israel has complicated U.S. attempts to play the role of a peace broker in Arab-Israeli conflict. After the failure of a U.S.-sponsored summit meeting in 2000 between Israeli prime minister Ehud Barak and the late Palestinian leader Yasir Arafat, the Bush administration cut off direct negotiations with the Palestinian leadership. In 2007, however, regional pressure on the Bush administration to restart the Israeli-Palestinian peace process increased. Jordan's King Abdullah II, in an address to Congress, called on the United States to use its influence for peace in what he termed the central conflict in the Middle East. In March 2007 member states of the Arab League, meeting in Saudi Arabia, renewed a proposal for peace with Israel based on justice for Palestinians. Israel responded with an offer to meet Arab leaders. However, the United States made no immediate move to bring the parties together.

Good Relations with Key Arab States

Despite its strong alliance with Israel, the United States has always maintained friendly relations with some key Arab states, even while it has battled others. Egypt has been a key U.S. friend in the Middle East, especially since 1978 when Egyptian president Anwar Sadat made a historic peace journey to Israel. Egypt has since become a major recipient of U.S. aid, trailing only Israel (and more recently Iraq). Currently, U.S. aid to Egypt exceeds $1 billion a year.

Jordan and Lebanon are also countries that have maintained officially friendly relations with America. In both countries, however, U.S. forces, diplomats, and citizens have faced terrorist attacks. Despite good relations with the government of Lebanon in the 1980s, Americans were driven from the country by kidnappings and terrorist attacks. Two notable instances occurred in its capital: In April 1983 a suicide bomber attacked the U.S. embassy in Beirut; months later, a truck bombing of U.S. Marines barracks killed 241 American soldiers. Afterward, President Ronald Reagan discreetly withdrew American forces from the country.

More recently, Jordan has proven to be a risky locale. In 2002, as the United States prepared to invade Iraq, a U.S. diplomat was assassinated in Jordan, and in 2005 terrorists launched deadly attacks on hotels in Amman, Jordan's capital city. Events there are emblematic of the new realities in the Middle East—even where the government is friendly, the environment may be hostile.

Special Ties to Saudi Arabia

Relations with the Kingdom of Saudi Arabia are unique. In many ways the norms of the kingdom are at odds with American values, but the two countries' governments are close and growing closer, due to the perceived threat of Iran. Saudi Arabia is dominated by an ultraconservative interpretation of Islam, known as Wahhabism. Women are not allowed to drive or to go out on their own. Major life decisions are made for them by male relatives. Ordinary people lack freedom of speech. However, the Saudis control the largest oil reserves in the world and have great influence over prices in the global petroleum market. They have also invested billions of dollars of their oil wealth in the United States. U.S. leaders therefore consider it important to maintain friendly relations with Saudi Arabia. Although deeply at odds over Israel, the two nations have found mutual interests in some regional issues. Saudi Arabia has cooperated in the fight against terrorism, especially since its own lands have become subject to terrorist attacks in recent years. Shiites are in control of Iran and predominant in the government of Iraq. To oppose the Shiites, Saudi Arabia has strengthened its alliance with the United States.

> " Shiites are in control of Iran and predominant in the government of Iraq. Saudi Arabia has strengthened its alliance with the United States. "

Most important to U.S. interests, in recent decades Saudi Arabia has acted to stabilize oil prices at times of crisis in the global markets. However, many analysts worry about the internal stability of the country. Ruled by a royal family and harsh Islamic law, the population is restive.

Despite the country's wealth, unemployment and discontent run high. Islamists hate their rulers' ties to the United States and are suspected of mounting attempts to overthrow them. Osama bin Laden, the world's most feared Islamist terrorist, is himself a Saudi who opposes the regime of his native country. Despite Saudi Arabia's powerful state security, terrorists have successfully launched a series of attacks against foreigners there. A revolution or coup in the country could be a disaster for the Western world, which remains dependent on oil for its economy. That is especially true for the United States, which ranks Saudi Arabia second only to Canada as a supplier of oil. Therefore, the U.S. government continues to strongly back the Saudi regime.

Middle East State Enemies

The United States considers some Middle Eastern countries to be "rogue states" that promote terrorism and constitute a threat to U.S. interests.

Libya was long on this list, although recently its leader, Mu'ammar Gadhafi, has made efforts to patch things up with the West by committing to end the use of terror. According to the U.S. State Department, Syria remains a brutal dictatorship that is suspected of sponsoring terrorist attacks and assassinations, especially in neighboring Lebanon.

At present, however, Iran stands as the most powerful state opposed to U.S. interests in the Middle East. Iran is quite different from the others on this list. The historical seat of Persian civilization, it is a non-Arab nation. It is also the only Shiite Muslim republic, putting it at odds with Sunni Muslim dominated countries such as Saudi Arabia. Iran is also partially democratic (the ruling clerics disqualify any candidates they find objectionable). Of greatest concern is the fact that Iran is developing nuclear materials that could be used to make nuclear weapons. Iran has defied United Nations' demands that it stop processing such materials. This leads to concerns that the United States may feel compelled to take military action against it. However, others question whether this is feasible, considering U.S. involvement in Iran's neighbor to the west.

Fresh Challenges for America

The 9/11 attacks and the costly miscalculations in Iraq point up new dilemmas for U.S. policy makers in the Middle East. On the one hand, America needs to defend its strategic interests in the region, principally access to oil, the alliance with Israel, and the suppression of Islamist terrorism. On the other hand, it has to find a way to meet its objectives without fueling the terrorism it seeks to extinguish or bankrupting its human and financial resources.

> **Most analysts, believe that the waves of violence in Iraq have turned into a civil war whose principal opponents are the Sunnis and Shiites.**

The challenge is evolving, however. The latest Middle East conundrum for the United States is the hostility between the two major sects of Islam, Sunni and Shia. Most analysts believe that the waves of violence in Iraq have turned into a civil war whose principal opponents are the Sunnis and Shiites. This has led to increased hostility between Sunnis and Shiites elsewhere. Martin Indyk, a former

U.S. ambassador to Israel, calls it a Sunni-Shiite Cold War. In particular, Saudi Arabia and Iran are at odds. Both nations are thought to be seeking nuclear weapons. Even short of that, the spread of sectarian conflict could seriously complicate an already complex situation.

The United States is in a bind. It supports the Shiite-led government of Iraq, but it is strongly allied with the Sunni-dominated countries of Saudi Arabia and Egypt. U.S. hostility to Iran dates back to the 1979 seizing of U.S. hostages from the American embassy in Tehran. However, U.S. policies support majority rule in a unified Iraq, and that means granting supreme power to Shiites in that country, which analysts say provides an enormous strategic boost to Iran.

The role of the United States remains pivotal in the region. However, its Arab allies face increasingly angry and restive populations, who resent America's support of Israel and its presence in Iraq. Iran is openly hostile to the United States and is increasingly asserting its dominance in the Middle East. In Afghanistan the extremist Taliban, which U.S. forces drove from power in 2001, is mounting attacks against international forces stationed there. Above all, however, the ongoing conflict in Iraq is costing lives and draining the U.S. Treasury. With American voters signaling that they favor an end to the U.S. presence in the midst of bloody conflict in Iraq, it appears that America's role in the Middle East is about to change again.

How Does U.S. Involvement Affect the Middle East?

“Our commitment to Iraq is long-term. But it is not a commitment to have our young men and women patrolling Iraq's streets open-endedly.”

—Robert Gates, quoted in Vince Crawley, "U.S. Troop Levels in Iraq Depend on Political Progress," Bureau of International Information Programs, U.S. Department of State, April 20, 2007. http://usinfo.state.gov.

Gates replaced Donald Rumsfeld as U.S. secretary of defense in late 2006.

“Iraq is in serious danger of coming apart because of lack of planning, underestimating the task and buying into a flawed strategy. . . . I don't know where the neocons came from. . . . Somehow, the neocons captured the president. They captured the vice president.”

—Anthony Zinni, quoted in Thomas E. Ricks, "For Vietnam Vet Anthony Zinni, Another War on Shaky Territory," *Washington Post,* December 23, 2003. www.washingtonpost.com.

Zinni was head of the U.S. Central Command until 2000.

* Editor's Note: While the definition of a primary source can be narrowly or broadly defined, for the purposes of Compact Research, a primary source consists of: 1) results of original research presented by an organization or researcher; 2) eyewitness accounts of events, personal experience, or work experience; 3) first-person editorials offering pundits' opinions; 4) government officials presenting political plans and/or policies; 5) representatives of organizations presenting testimony or policy.

66 We've got a chance to resist Iranian push into the region, but we better get about it. I mean, it's not the sort of thing that you can just let continue in its current form. It's why you have to resist Hezbollah. . . . It's why you have to resist the Damascus Hamas, creating a situation in the Palestinian territories where moderates can emerge. It is why in the final analysis a stable Shia-led but not dominated government in Iraq is at the core of all of this. 99

—Condoleezza Rice, "Interview with the Wall Street Journal Editorial Board,"
Department of State, September 25, 2006. www.state.gov.

Rice served as secretary of state in the second term of the George W. Bush administration.

66 One might assume that the bond between the two countries [Israel and the United States] is based on shared strategic interests or compelling moral imperatives. . . . Instead, the overall thrust of U.S. policy in the region is due almost entirely to U.S. domestic politics, and especially to the activities of the 'Israel Lobby.' 99

—John Mearsheimer and Stephen Walt, "The Israel Lobby and U.S. Foreign
Policy," *London Review of Books,* March 23, 2006.

Mearsheimer is the R. Wendell Harrison Distinguished Service Professor of Political Science at the University of Chicago. Walt is the Robert and Renee Belfer Professor of International Affairs at the John F. Kennedy School of Government at Harvard University.

66 The Middle East is heading into a serious Sunni-Shiite Cold War. 99

—Martin Indyk, quoted in Seymour M. Hersh, "The Redirection," *New Yorker,* March 5, 2007.

Indyk was ambassador to Israel during the Clinton administration.

❝If the United States says that discussions with the likes of us can be useful . . . in determining American policy in the region, we have no objection to talks or meetings. But if their aim . . . is to impose their policy on us, it will be a waste of time.❞

—Hassan Nasrallah, quoted in Seymour M. Hersh, "The Redirection," *New Yorker,* March 5, 2007.

Nasrallah is the leader of the Shiite Lebanese organization Hizballah.

❝At the start, some believed that the Americans were help-ing them. There wasn't any hatred toward the Ameri-cans. After what has happened in Iraq, there is an un-precedented hatred and the Americans know it. There exists today a hatred never equaled in the region.❞

Hosni Mubarak, quoted in *Boston Globe,* "Egypt's Leader Says Arabs Hate US More than Ever," April 21, 2004. www.boston.com.

Mubarak, the president of Egypt, is one of America's closest allies in the Middle East.

❝Does Israel have supporters in the U.S. that back a strong relationship between the two countries? Clear-ly, networks of such support exist, as they do for U.S. ties with Britain, Greece, Turkey, and India. There are also states like Saudi Arabia that have tried to tilt U.S. policy using a vast array of powerful PR firms, former diplomats, and well-connected officials.❞

—Dore Gold, "The Basis of the U.S.-Israel Alliance: An Israeli Response to the Mearsheimer-Walt Assault," *Jerusalem Issue Brief,* March, 24 2006. www.jcpa.org.

Gold is president of the Jerusalem Center for Public Affairs. He was the eleventh Permanent Representative of Israel to the United Nations.

---

66 It is my belief that the Bible Belt in America is Israel's only safety belt right now. 99

—Jerry Falwell, quoted in *CBS News,* "Zion's Christian Soldiers," June 8, 2003. www.cbsnews.com.

Falwell was an evangelical television preacher who founded the politically active Moral Majority.

66 Arguments that Israel's existence will be endangered if U.S. military aid is eliminated are specious. Israel has 200 nuclear weapons that ultimately guarantee its security vis-a-vis neighboring Arab countries, none of which are nuclear powers. Furthermore, Israel is at peace with Egypt—its largest and most dangerous neighbor. 99

—Ivan Eland, "U.S. Policy Harms Prospects for Middle East Peace," *Independent Institute Commentary,* November 22, 2004. www.independent.org.

Eland is director of the Center on Peace & Liberty at the Independent Institute.

66 The friendship and cooperation between our [U.S. and Saudi] governments and peoples are precious jewels whose value we should never underestimate. 99

—Ronald Reagan, quoted in *Washington Times,* "Saudi-U.S. Relations: A Future of Steady Growth," September 22, 2000. www.internationalspecialreports.com.

Reagan was the fortieth president of the United States.

66 **The underpinning of the relationship is the human ties, and they [ties between Saudis and Americans] are frayed to the point of non-existence.** 99

—Chas Freeman, quoted in Barbara Slavin, "Saudi-U.S. Human Ties Are Fraying in Post-9/11 World," *USA Today,* June 21, 2005. www.usatoday.com.

Freeman was U.S. ambassador to Saudi Arabia during the 1991 Gulf War.

66 **The threat to the political and economic world posed by Saudi instability I think is greater than the threat that was posed by Iraq.** 99

—Richard Clarke, quoted in CNN.com, "Clarke: Saudi Instability More Worrying than Iraq," June 9, 2004. http://cnn.worldnews.com.

Clarke was an antiterrorism adviser to the White House in both the Clinton and second Bush administrations.

66 **American policy in our region has resulted in the displacement of 4 million Palestinians and 9 million Iraqis—isn't that enough for the American administration to realize that they look and act in complete darkness?** 99

—Bouthaina Shaaban, "A Shared Vision Between Rice and Peretz: Total Darkness," *Asharq Alawsat,* February 26, 2007. www.asharq-e.com.

Shaaban is minister of expatriates in Syria and professor of English literature at the University of Damascus.

How Does U.S. Involvement Affect the Middle East?

- More than **100,000 U.S. troops** have been deployed to Iraq since 2003. At times the number has gone as high as 150,000.

- Another **100,000 U.S. troops** are stationed in other parts of the Middle East, including Kuwait, Turkey, and Saudi Arabia.

- Since World War II the United States has been the **leading provider of aid** to its strategic friends and allies in the Middle East region.

- The United States is the **leading provider of arms** to the Middle East. More than **$2 billion** a year in U.S. military aid goes to Israel; and more than **$1 billion** in arms sales go to Arab countries including Egypt, Saudi Arabia, and the Gulf states.

- The United States used to support Iraq's late dictator **Saddam Hussein.** That policy changed when Saddam launched an invasion of Kuwait in 1990.

- The U.S. invasion of Iraq in 2003 has been its costliest intervention in the Middle East. The bill to American taxpayers exceeds **$400 billion** and is rising by more than **$2 billion a week.**

U.S. Foreign Aid and Human Development

Seven of the top 10 countries receiving U.S. aid are in the greater Middle East. Iraq has lately surpassed Israel as the top aid recipient.

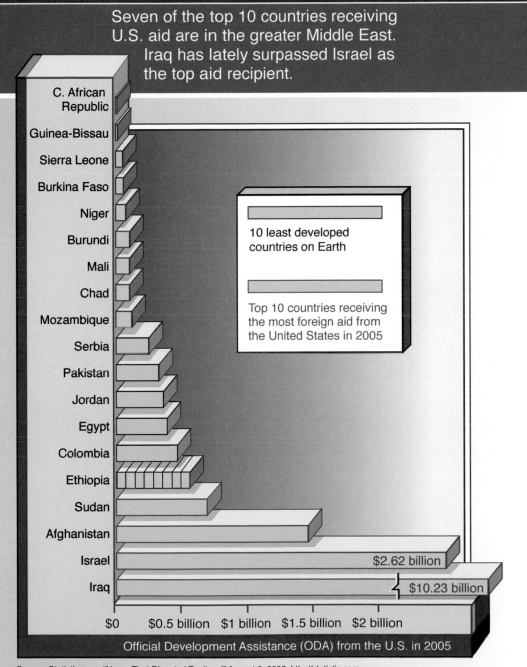

10 least developed countries on Earth

Top 10 countries receiving the most foreign aid from the United States in 2005

C. African Republic
Guinea-Bissau
Sierra Leone
Burkina Faso
Niger
Burundi
Mali
Chad
Mozambique
Serbia
Pakistan
Jordan
Egypt
Colombia
Ethiopia
Sudan
Afghanistan
Israel — $2.62 billion
Iraq — $10.23 billion

$0 $0.5 billion $1 billion $1.5 billion $2 billion

Official Development Assistance (ODA) from the U.S. in 2005

Source: Statistic.com, "Name That Disputed Territory!" August 8, 2006. http://statistic.com.

Sources of U.S. Oil Imports in 2005

The United States is the world's leading oil importer, with nearly one-fifth of its supply coming from the Middle East, where tension and instability are widespread.

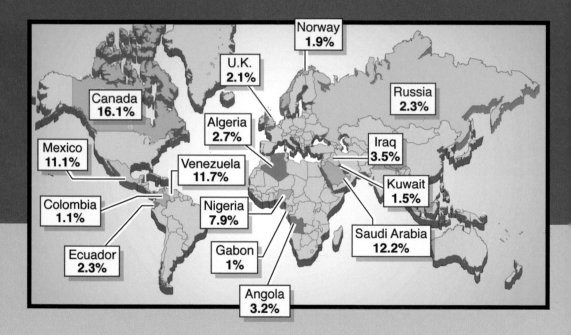

Norway
1.9%

U.K.
2.1%

Russia
2.3%

Canada
16.1%

Algeria
2.7%

Iraq
3.5%

Mexico
11.1%

Venezuela
11.7%

Kuwait
1.5%

Colombia
1.1%

Nigeria
7.9%

Saudi Arabia
12.2%

Ecuador
2.3%

Gabon
1%

Angola
3.2%

Source: Ariel Cohen, "Reducing U.S. Dependence on Middle Eastern Oil, Backgrounder #1926, April 7, 2006. www.heritage.org.

- The United States has **no diplomatic relations** with Iran. Relations were broken off in 1979 when radical students, with the support of the Iranian government, took over the U.S. embassy in Tehran and seized American hostages.

- The U.S. invasion of Iraq has caused public opinion of America to decline sharply not only in Muslim countries but in Europe and Asia as well. According to U.S. State Department surveys, only in Great Britain, Japan, India, and Nigeria do the majority of people hold a favorable opinion of the United States.

Arab Investments in the United States Are Rising

Oil-rich Arab countries invest significant amounts in the United States but often run into controversy. In 2006, when Dubai bought a company that operated six U.S. ports, the U.S. Congress forced a resale to an American company.

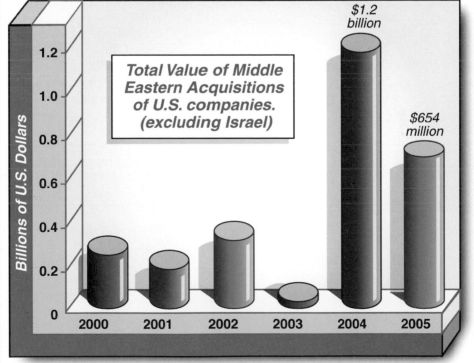

Total Value of Middle Eastern Acquisitions of U.S. companies. (excluding Israel)

Source: Paul Blustein, "Mideast Investment Up in U.S.: Proposed Ports Deal Is Just Part of Flood of Oil Wealth Spilling Ashore," *Washington Post*, March 7, 2006. www.washingtonpost.com.

Global U.S. Troop Deployment

U.S. troop deployment to the Middle East has risen sharply since the 2003 invasion of Iraq. As of 2007, more than 200,000 U.S. service men and women are stationed in the Middle East.

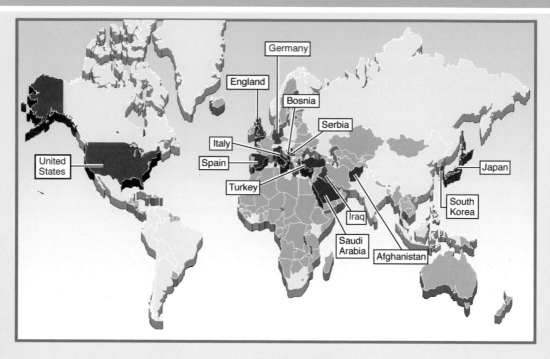

From 2000 to 2005

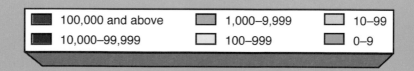

100,000 and above	1,000–9,999	10–99
10,000–99,999	100–999	0–9

Source: Tim Kane, "Global U.S. Troop Deployment, 1950–2003," Heritage Foundation, October 27, 2004. www.heritage.org.

How Does the Arab-Israeli Conflict Affect the Middle East?

66 We will never recognize Israel. There is nothing called Israel, neither in reality nor in the imagination. 99

—Hamas official Nizar Rayyan, *New York Times.*

66 [Palestinian Prime Minister Ismail] Haniyeh transferred over a million dollars for . . . terrorist actions against Israeli citizens. He's a terrorist. You have a terrorist who is prime minister of the Palestinian Authority now. 99

—Israeli Prime Minister Ehud Olmert, *Time.*

Two peoples, one land. That is the essence of the long and bloody dispute between Palestinians and Israelis. It is a conflict that has affected global politics and economics for decades. At times each has denied the other's right to exist as a nation, and even now there are many on either side of the divide who express a wish to annihilate the other. At times peace has seemed tantalizingly close, only to slip away. In 2007, as the United States and other major powers started yet another initiative for peace, the disagreements between the two peoples seemed as bitter and irreconcilable as ever.

Israeli Grievances

From the Israeli point of view, the United Nations partition plan, which set the international framework for the creation of Israel, designated a modest amount of territory for a long-promised Jewish homeland. From the moment Israel declared independence in 1948, the Arab nations around it declared war. Israel argues that the unyielding hostility of many of its neighbors has forced it to take unceasing steps to ensure the survival of the Jewish state. These include fighting and winning four major regional wars and forcefully resisting Palestinian terrorism and cross-border attacks from Islamic militias. Israel believes it has repeatedly demonstrated its willingness to make peace with its neighbors and, since 1993, with the Palestinians. Israel has given back major portions of land it captured in war in return for peace treaties with Egypt and Jordan. Despite numerous attempts to make peace with Palestinians, Israel continues to suffer horrific attacks on civilians by Palestinians and other Arabs who reject Israel's very right to exist. In 2006 Palestinians elected a government whose party leaders reject the very existence of Israel. Under the constant threat of attack, Israel refuses to negotiate with Palestinians until the violence is halted and the leadership acknowledges Israel's right to exist within secure borders.

> "Israel believes it has repeatedly demonstrated its willingness to make peace with its neighbors.

Palestinian Grievances

From the Palestinian point of view, the creation of Israel was a catastrophe imposed on them by Western nations that felt guilty about the Nazi genocide of European Jews. Hundreds of thousands of Palestinian Arabs fled their homes during Israel's 1948 War of Independence. In some instances Zionist paramilitary groups, such as the Irgun, waged terrorist campaigns to drive them out. The Palestinians thus became refugees and the newly minted Israeli citizens took over their land and homes. Ignored by the world for decades, some Palestinians turned to terrorism to bring attention to their plight and pressure Israel to change its policies, while others pursued peaceful resistance. Palestinians lament that they have all been stereotyped as terrorists, while the role of Jewish terrorism in the formation of Israel is conveniently forgotten. Moreover, they say, the current actions of the Israeli Defense Forces amount to deadly state terrorism against Palestinian civilians. Meantime, Israel's support of Jewish settlers is forcing millions of Palestinians to live in ever-shrinking territories.

Unrelenting Terrorism Against Israel

Palestinian militants have long resorted to terrorism in the attempt to intimidate or coerce Israel. In pursuit of their cause Palestinian militants made themselves the international emblem of terrorism, surpassed only by al Qaeda after 9/11.

They changed forever the way international events are staged with an assault on the 1972 summer Olympics in Munich, West Germany. Members of a Palestinian terrorist group broke into the Israeli athletes' compound at the Olympics, killed 2 members of the Israeli delegation, and took 9 others hostage. The assault ended days later in a wild firefight in which all the hostages and all but 3 of the 8 kidnappers were killed. Ever since, security has been a major part of event planning around the world.

Beginning in 1993 Palestinians began a sporadic campaign of suicide bombing in Israel. Despite the occasional bombings, attempts at normalization continued through the 1990s; and for a time hundreds of thousands of Palestinians commuted daily into Israel to work, while Israeli tourists visited sites in Palestinian territories. In the fall of 2000, however, a new wave of Palestinian violence, often referred to as the Second Intifada (translated as "uprising"), brought peaceful interactions to an end. Suicide bombings proliferated, killing a least 1,000 Israelis by the end of 2002 and wounding thousands more. Israel reports that Palestinian terrorist attacks against its people, while remaining intense, have fallen from a high of 7,634 incidents in 2001 to 2,135 in 2006.

The psychological toll of Palestinian suicide bombing is enormous. The bombings make the assumption of normality impossible. Israeli journalist and author David Horovitz describes how even a university attended by several thousand Arabs was targeted. "The bomber . . . was a Palestinian painter working

> " While the Palestinians became refugees, newly minted Israeli citizens took over their land and homes. "

on campus, and he knew full well . . . that he risked killing both Jews and Muslims. If all those who strive to kill and maim the innocent have forsaken their humanity, what words are left with which to revile murderers whose indifference extends to the suffering of their own kin?"[4]

> The psychological toll of Palestinian suicide bombing is enormous. It makes the assumption of normality impossible.

For all its fury, the Palestinian war of terrorism has yielded few if any tangible results for its people. Israel's stance continues to be that it will not negotiate a comprehensive settlement unless such violence is first halted. In the meantime, it is proceeding with a unilateral disengagement plan to seal itself off from its angry and often murderous neighbors.

Settlements in Occupied Territories

One of the most contentious issues concerning the Palestinians and Israelis is the network of Jewish settlements throughout the Occupied Territories. Following the 1967 Six Day War, Israeli military forces occupied the Sinai Peninsula, Gaza Strip, West Bank, Golan Heights, and all of Jerusalem. At first Israel's policy was to prevent its citizens from settling in those zones. Beginning in the 1970s, however, illegal Jewish settlements began to take root, and subsequently the Israeli government reversed policy and began to support settlement throughout the Occupied Territories.

As of 2007 at least 130 Jewish settlements remain in the West Bank. Some 220,000 Israelis live in the West Bank, out of approximately 400,000 settlers in all. Even the total number is a relatively small proportion—less than 10 percent—of the more than 5 million Jewish citizens of Israel. However, the infrastructure that supports the settlements takes up far more territory claimed by the Palestinians than the settlements themselves. The government has built a network of "Israeli only" highways connecting settlements with the Israeli homeland. These heavily guarded roads isolate Palestinian communities from one another. Each settlement is surrounded by a "security zone" administered by the government. According to the Foundation for Middle East Peace, each of the security zones surrounding the more than 150 West Bank settlements has an average perimeter of 4 miles.

Palestinians complain that not only do the settlements carve up their territory, but security zones have led to the wholesale uprooting of millions of their olive trees. Olives are a staple of the Palestinian diet. Israel points to the frequent Palestinian attacks on settlements as justifying its security measures. After one assault in which Palestinian militants fired antitank weapons and mortar rounds at a Jewish settlement, Israeli government spokesman David Baker said, "Israel is obliged to provide security for its citizens and will take the necessary defensive measures if the Palestinian Authority continues to persist in this path."[5]

Compounding the issue of Jewish settlements is the question of land ownership. The Israeli civic group Peace Now claims that the settlements and their security zones are being built largely on privately owned Palestinian land. Using data obtained from the government, the group issued a report in late 2006 concluding that 40 percent of the land used for settlements rightfully belongs in private Palestinian hands.

Greater Israel and the International Response

Jewish settlements in the Occupied Territories have been inspired largely by the vision of a "Greater Israel." In contrast to the thin strip of land delineated for Israel by the United Nations partition plan, advocates of Greater Israel want to see the state exert sovereignty over all the land of Israel described in the Bible.

These include the provinces known in ancient times as Judea and Samaria—lands that today make up the West Bank. Israel has not asserted sovereignty over the West Bank—indeed, it has offered to give much of it up for peace—but critics charge that since the mid-1970s, government support for settlements has been aimed at building "facts on the ground"* that would permanently integrate the West Bank settlements into Israel proper.

The British group Christian Aid claims that Israel's settlement policies amount to "shorthand for large-scale de facto expropriation of land"[6]

---

* The phrase, which has become commonplace in Israeli politics, is attributed to Israeli defense minister Moshe Dayan, who spoke of the need for settlement following Israel's victory in the 1967 war.

from the Palestinians. Opponents of Israel's settlement policy argue that it is illegal under international law. They point to various United Nations resolutions, especially U.N. Resolution 242, passed in the aftermath of the 1967 Six Day War, which calls for the "withdrawal of Israeli armed forces from territories occupied in the recent conflict."[7]

Interpretation of this clause has been widely disputed, but most nations, including the United States, have interpreted it to mean that Israel should not build permanent settlements in the Occupied Territories.

Fencing In Settlements, Fencing Out Bombers

In 2004 both U.S. and Israeli policies on settlements appeared to shift. President George W. Bush, in a letter to Israeli prime minister Ariel Sharon, stated that peace plans should take account of "new realities on the ground, including already existing major Israeli population centers."[8] It would be unrealistic, Bush wrote, to expect Israel to abandon all its settlements as part of a negotiated peace.

At the same time, Sharon announced a policy of unilateral disengagement from the Palestinians. This involves abandonment of settlements in Gaza, from which Israel has subsequently withdrawn. In the West Bank, however, Israel remains committed to its major settlements. Israel has undertaken the construction of what it calls a security fence to protect itself from West Bank assailants.

Critics charge that the barrier is creating a new, permanent border that adds the majority of the West Bank settler population to Israel's territory. Former U.S. president Jimmy Carter goes so far as to charge that Israel is creating apartheid in the West Bank, which he describes as the forced separation and "total domination and oppression of Palestinians by the dominant Israeli military."[9] The Israeli Ministry of Foreign Affairs strongly denies such charges. It states that the fence is a temporary and purely defensive measure. It points to a rapid decline in the number of successful suicide bombings since construction on the barrier began. Between 2000 and 2003, 73 suicide bombings originated in the West Bank; from 2003 through 2006, only 12 succeeded, according to a March 2007 report issued by Israel's Intelligence and Terrorism Information Center.

Effects on Israel

Having held the upper hand in its conflicts with Palestinians and their Arab allies for more than 50 years, Israel has gained in some ways. Thanks to victory in war its territory is considerably larger than what the original United Nations partition plan mapped out. Thanks to U.S. aid amounting to billions of dollars annually, its economy remains prosperous despite a heavy defense burden. Although Israel remains vulnerable to occasional militia or terrorist attacks, its security is much more assured than in the past. A peace treaty with Egypt, once the most formidable of its Arab opponents, has proven durable for three decades. Jordan has also reached an accommodation with Israel. Iraq, a hostile foe under Saddam Hussein, has been plunged into internal conflict by the 2003 U.S. invasion. Israel faces little effective opposition to its plans to isolate the Palestinians from Israel by fencing them out. And although terrorist attacks continue, the number of suicide bombings has fallen steeply since a peak in 2002.

> **Israel has undertaken the construction of what it calls a security fence to protect itself from West Bank assailants.**

However, critics within and outside Israel charge that in achieving victory the nation has abandoned its commitment to equality and human rights. While acknowledging that Palestinians launched numerous deadly attacks against Israelis, the U.S. State Department's 2006 Human Rights Report documents a wide variety of abuses committed by Israeli Defense Forces (IDF) and settlers against Palestinians. "Israeli forces continued to use Palestinians as 'human shields' in violation of Israeli law despite High Court rulings in 2002 and 2005,"[10] the report notes. It also records that Palestinians are abused and humiliated at Israeli checkpoints and that IDF military operations led to the deaths of 660 Palestinians in the Occupied Territories during 2006. Such tactics have led to widespread criticism of Israel, even among those who support it. "At some point," writes Pulitzer prize–winning journalist Richard Ben Cramer, "Israel ground away, or gave away, her birthright of loyalty from the West."[11] Others, however, regard Israel's response to the onslaught of terror attacks as remarkably courageous.

Effects on the Palestinians

Decades of frustration, poverty, and hopelessness have had a profoundly demoralizing effect on the Palestinians. They live in worsening poverty and overcrowding. Those in the West Bank often have to spend hours at Israeli checkpoints just to travel from home to work or town to town. Those living in the Gaza Strip are largely cut off from the rest of the world, including their fellow Palestinians in the West Bank. Since 2000, Israel's security crackdown has contributed to economic hardships that have left the Palestinians the poorest of the Arab peoples. Per capita income in the Palestinian territories is estimated at about $1,700 a year.

Self-government has been largely a failure. Corruption was reportedly so widespread in the Fatah administration that almost nothing got done without a bribe. Millions in foreign aid failed to reach the people it was meant for. In 2006 the Palestinian people reacted by throwing out the Fatah party and electing the Islamist party Hamas to lead their government. This, however, has worsened their plight in many respects. Hamas has refused to recognize Israel and clashed with Fatah. In June 2007 the Palestinian Authority split, with Hamas ruling Gaza, and Fatah predominant in the West Bank. While some international aid began to flow to Fatah, the internal conflict has worsened the Palestinians' economic and social hardships.

> **Critics within and outside Israel charge that in achieving victory the nation has abandoned its commitment to equality and human rights.**

Finally, the human toll of conflict has fallen especially hard on the Palestinians. In the current phase of uprising against Israel, which began in 2000, about four times as many Palestinians as Israelis have died, according to figures from the respective governments.

Regional and the World Effects

The repeated failures to defeat Israel in war have left the Arab nations angry, their governments vulnerable, and the region unstable. Having made a separate peace with Israel in 1978, Egypt now enjoys enormous aid subsidies from the United States, amounting to more than $1 billion annually, but faces the constant threat of Islamic terror from within. Traditionally one of the most open of Arab societies,

Egypt has taken repressive measures in the pursuit of national security.

Jordan, which has also made peace with Israel, faces instability because a large portion of its population is composed of restive Palestinians. The country's hereditary leader, King Abdullah II, regards settlement of the Israeli-Palestinian conflict as key to peace throughout the region and is leading an effort to restart the dormant peace process.

Lebanon, another relatively open society, has been torn apart, first by civil war, then by Israeli and Syrian occupation. In 2006 it suffered extensive damage when Israel's air force, seeking to knock out Iranian-backed Hizballah guerrilla units that were launching missiles into its territory, bombed virtually the entire country.

Nearly all the other Arab countries have harsh, repressive regimes that are made unstable by discontented populations. Even Saudi Arabia, despite its oil wealth, has been unable to placate its young people, some of whom have turned to terrorism.

The entire world has felt the consequences. For several decades, starting in the early 1970s, Palestinian terrorists carried out attacks in Europe, South America, and on the high seas. The Arab-Israeli conflict has buffeted world oil markets on numerous occasions, and Middle East tensions continue to affect world energy prices today. Finally, the United States, Europe, and Russia have poured billions of dollars and much prestige into attempts to bring about a lasting settlement of the disputes. Despite some progress, much of the aid and effort have been wasted. In short, the central conflict in the Middle East has been bad for all parties, yet the path to a just and lasting peace has remained elusive.

> **Traditionally one of the most open of Arab societies, Egypt has taken repressive measures in the pursuit of national security.**

How Does the Arab-Israeli Conflict Affect the Middle East?

66 We firmly stand by the historic right of the people of Israel to the entire Land of Israel. Every hill in Samaria and every valley in Judea is part of our historic homeland. 99

—Ehud Olmert, quoted in Joel Leyden, "Olmert Herzliya Conference Speech: Disengagement Continues," Israel News Agency, January 24, 2006. www.israelnewsagency.com.

Olmert took over the duties of prime minister in early 2006 after Prime Minister Ariel Sharon fell into a coma following a stroke.

66 There can be no erasing of the historical truth that the existence of Israel is predicated, indeed imposed upon, the obliteration of another society and people. 99

—Edward Said, "The Challenge of Israel: Fifty Years On," *Al-Ahram,* January 1998. http://weekly.ahram.org.eg.

Said was a professor of humanities at Columbia University and a noted spokesman for the Palestinian people.

Bracketed quotes indicate conflicting positions.

* Editor's Note: While the definition of a primary source can be narrowly or broadly defined, for the purposes of Compact Research, a primary source consists of: 1) results of original research presented by an organization or researcher; 2) eyewitness accounts of events, personal experience, or work experience; 3) first-person editorials offering pundits' opinions; 4) government officials presenting political plans and/or policies; 5) representatives of organizations presenting testimony or policy.

66 The anti-terrorist fence is a temporary, defensive measure—not a border; the border is to be determined by direct negotiations between Israel and the Palestinians. 99

— Israeli Ministry of Foreign Affairs, "Saving Lives: Israel's Anti-Terrorist Fence—Answers to Questions," January 1, 2004. www.mfa.gov.il.

The Israeli Ministry of Foreign Affairs is responsible for the country's relations with other nations.

66 Under the pretext of security, Israel is continuing to carry out, through the Apartheid Wall, its long-term policy of occupation, discrimination and expulsion that amounts to ethnic cleansing and to the destruction of the material basis for the survival and development of Palestinian society as a whole. 99

—PENGON, "Stop Israel's Siege and Attacks on Gaza; Stop the Environmental and Humanitarian Disaster," July 18, 2006. www.pengon.org.

PENGON is a coalition of nongovernmental environmental organizations supporting the Palestinian cause.

66 Where the Palestinians want liberation, Israeli Jews want secure borders. Given the atrocities that have scarred Jewish history, this is hardly surprising. . . . But walls are no good if there is deadly trouble within. 99

Karen Armstrong, *Jerusalem: One City, Three Faiths.* New York: Ballantine, 1998.

Armstrong is a former nun and a leading author on religious affairs.

❝Under the roadmap, Palestinians must undertake an immediate cessation of armed activity and all acts of violence against Israelis anywhere, and all official Palestinian institutions must end incitement against Israel.❞

—George W. Bush, "Letter to Prime Minister Sharon," April 14, 2004. www.fmep.org.

Bush is the forty-third president of the United States.

❝The Palestinian people are left with no option but to revolt, as costly and uncertain as it has been throughout the years. Thus, it must be stated that Palestinian resistance, which for the most part has been a nonviolent and popular movement, shall continue as long as the circumstances that contributed to its commencement remain in place.❞

—Ramzy Baroud, "Middle East Peace Process: Stagnation by Design," *Global Research,* December 23, 2006. www.pengon.org.

Baroud is an Arab American journalist and author of *The Second Palestinian Intifada: A Chronicle of a People's Struggle.*

❝Islamic society always threw a web over men that restrained them, but the European Zionists came out of a different culture and faith and they were not shackled by any webs. That was how they made a state. The Sephardim, the Arab Jews, never could have built Israel. They would have had coffee with the Palestinians instead.❞

—Thomas Friedman, *From Beirut to Jerusalem.* New York: Anchor, 1990.

Friedman is a columnist for the *New York Times.*

66 This war will not end, and anyone who deludes himself that there will be peace must understand that Israel did not come to this region to love the Arabs or to normalize relations with them. . . . Either we will exist or we will not exist. Either the Israelis or the Palestinians—there is no third option. **99**

—Adel Sadeq, interview by Iqraa TV, April 23, 2002, quoted in Likoed Nederland. www.likud.nl.

Sadeq is head of the department of psychiatry at Ein Shams University in Cairo and recipient of the 1990 Egyptian State Prize.

66 Many people speak about a viable Palestinian state, but we also have to think about a *viable Jewish state.* For the Jewish state to be viable, it must be defendable. Without being able to defend ourselves, we cannot have a viable state, whether or not there is a peace agreement. That is why Israelis are so concerned about security arrangements. **99**

—Yuval Steinitz, "The Growing Threat to Israel's Qualitative Military Edge," *Jerusalem Issue Brief,* December 11, 2003. www.jcpa.org.

Steinitz is chairman of the Foreign Affairs and Defense Committee of the Knesset, Israel's parliament.

66 This country exists as the fulfillment of a promise made by God Himself. It would be ridiculous to ask it to account for its legitimacy. **99**

—Golda Meir, interview by *Le Monde,* October 15, 1971, quoted in MonaBaker.com. www.monabaker.com.

Meir was prime minister of Israel from 1969 until 1974.

❝It is inconceivable that Israel will become a legitimate state even if the peace process is implemented.❞

—Bashar Al-Assad, interview by Talal Salman, *Al-Safir,* March 27, 2003. www.memri.org.

Assad is president of Syria.

❝Resuming the Arab-Israeli peace process is not a matter of forcing concessions from Israel or dragooning the Palestinians into surrender. . . . What is required is to summon the will of Arab and Israeli leaders, led by a determined American president, to forge the various elements into a conclusion that all parties have already publicly accepted in principle.❞

—Brent Scowcroft, "Getting the Middle East Back on Our Side," *New York Times,* January 4, 2007. www.nytimes.com.

Scowcroft served as national security advisor under Presidents Gerald R. Ford and George H.W. Bush.

❝There are certain conditions, according to Jewish law, under which non-Jews may live here. This doesn't apply to the Arabs. They don't fit the category. They have to get the hell out.❞

—Shmuel ben Yishai, quoted in PBS, "Israel's Next War?" *Frontline,* April 5, 2005. www.pbs.org.

Ben Yishai is an Israeli settler in Hebron.

❝The United States is squandering international prestige and goodwill and intensifying global anti-American terrorism by unofficially condoning or abetting the Israeli confiscation and colonization of Palestinian territories.❞

—Jimmy Carter, *Palestine: Peace Not Apartheid.* New York: Simon and Schuster, 2006.

Carter was the thirty-ninth president of the United States and won the 2002 Nobel Peace Prize for his peacemaking efforts in the Middle East.

---

66 Evangelical Christians support Israel because we believe that the words of Moses and the ancient prophets of Israel were inspired by God. We believe that the emergence of a Jewish state in the land promised by God to Abraham, Isaac, and Jacob was ordained by God. We believe that God has a plan for this nation which He intends to be a blessing to all the nations of the earth. 99

—Pat Robertson, "Why Evangelical Christians Support Israel," Herzliya Conference, Lauder School of Government, Diplomacy, and Strategy, December 17, 2003. www.patrobertson.com.

Robertson is the founder and chairman of the Christian Broadcasting Network.

66 Settlements, Jewish communities that were established in the West Bank and Gaza Strip after the territories were gained in the 1967 War, do not violate international law. . . . Neither Jordan nor Egypt had legal sovereignty over these areas. . . . Jews have lived in the West Bank and Gaza Strip throughout recorded history, until 1948 when they were forced to flee the invading Arab armies. Indeed, several of the current settlement communities existed prior to 1948 when they where overrun by invading Arab armies. 99

—Anti-Defamation League, "How to Respond to Common Misstatements About Israel," March 14, 2007. www.adl.org.

The Anti-Defamation League, founded in 1913, works to combat anti-Semitism and bigotry.

66 One can't really accuse Israel of violating the Oslo agreements, except in detail. It continued to settle the occupied territories and integrate them within Israel. That means you and I did it, because the U.S. funds it knowingly, and the U.S. provides crucial diplomatic and military support for these gross violations of international law. 99

—Noam Chomsky, "Prospects for Peace in the Middle East," lecture at the University of Toledo, March 4, 2001. www.zmag.org.

Chomsky is a linguistics scholar and social critic.

How Does the Arab-Israeli Conflict Affect the Middle East?

- The land that Palestinians and Israelis contend over has been continuously occupied throughout history. It was Canaan, then Judea and Samaria, the home of the Jews, and was subsequently conquered by the Romans and **renamed Palestine.**

- The population of Israel is about **6.5 million,** of whom about **230,000** live in settlements in the Occupied Territories.

- The population of the Palestinians in the Occupied Territories (also known as the West Bank and Gaza Strip) is about **4 million,** with another **5 million Palestinians** living elsewhere in the region and around the world.

- Israel receives **$2.1 billion** in U.S. military aid annually and another $600 million in economic aid.

- In 1998 various Western countries pledged nearly **$4 billion** in aid to help Palestinians as part of a peace settlement. However, much of that aid has been held up, either by the donors or by Israel, because of renewed Palestinian violence.

- Israel faces terrorist attacks from a number of **Palestinian organizations.** One of these, Hamas, gained a majority in the Palestinian parliament in 2006.

- Palestinians have been squeezed into steadily shrinking territories since 1948, while their population has grown from **730,000** to more than **4 million.**

- More than **1,000 Israelis** have been killed in terrorist attacks since 2000.

- In the same period, more than **4,000 Palestinians** have died as the result of Israeli police or military actions.

Palestinians Live in Shrinking Territories

Since 1947, the Palestinians have been squeezed into shrinking territories even while their population has more than quadrupled. While historical and present ownership of land remains hotly disputed, the territory controlled and occupied by Palestinians has dwindled since the establishment of Israel.

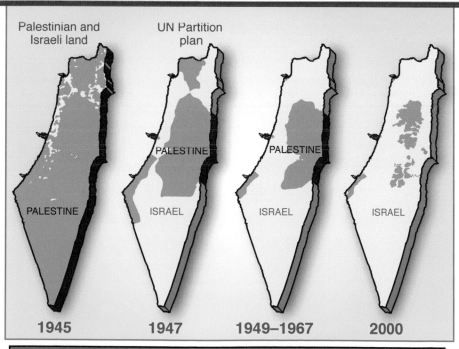

Palestinian and Israeli land | UN Partition plan

1945   1947   1949–1967   2000

Israeli Land   Palestinian Land

Source: thepeoplesvoice.org, "Zionists and the Land," May 15, 2006.
www.thepeoplesvoice.org.

Accords Have Failed to Stem the Growth of Israeli Settlements

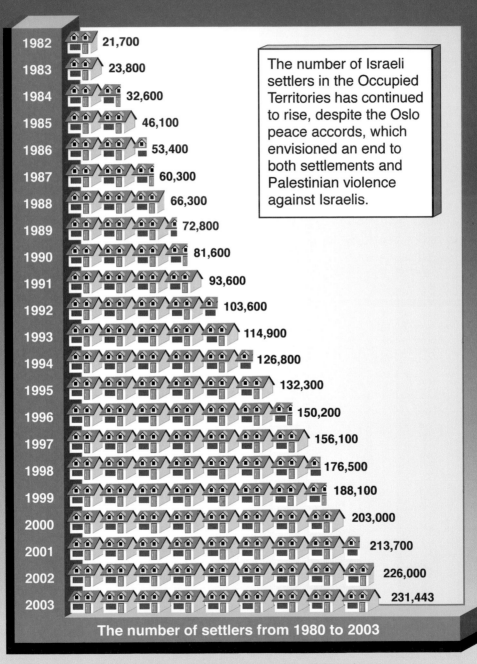

The number of Israeli settlers in the Occupied Territories has continued to rise, despite the Oslo peace accords, which envisioned an end to both settlements and Palestinian violence against Israelis.

Year	Number of settlers
1982	21,700
1983	23,800
1984	32,600
1985	46,100
1986	53,400
1987	60,300
1988	66,300
1989	72,800
1990	81,600
1991	93,600
1992	103,600
1993	114,900
1994	126,800
1995	132,300
1996	150,200
1997	156,100
1998	176,500
1999	188,100
2000	203,000
2001	213,700
2002	226,000
2003	231,443

The number of settlers from 1980 to 2003

Source: Haaretz.com, "New Year Supplement: The Price of the Settlements," 2003. www.haaretz.com.

Territories Occupied by Israel Since 1967

Following its victory in the 1967 Six Day War, Israel took control of territories known as the Sinai Peninsula, the Gaza Strip, the West Bank, and the Golan Heights. It has since returned the Sinai to Egypt as part of a peace treaty, and is in the process of withdrawing unilaterally from the Gaza Strip.

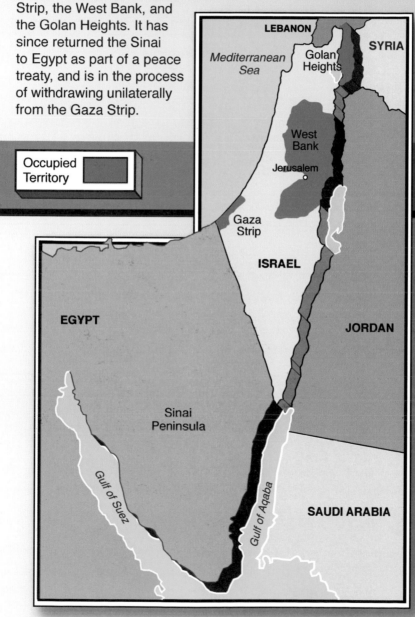

Occupied Territory

Source: Friends Committee on National Legislation, "The Israeli-Palestinian Conflict: Requirements for a Just, Secure, and Lasting Peace," *FCNL Perspectives,* March 2003. www.fcnl.org.

As Security Fence Goes Up, Suicide Bombings Dwindle

Although attempts continue, successful Palestinian suicide bombing attacks against Israel have fallen rapidly since Israel began construction of a barrier intended to keep out would-be bombers from the Palestinian territories.

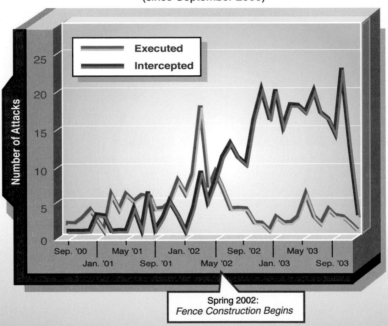

Suicide Bomber Attacks
(since September 2000)

Spring 2002:
Fence Construction Begins

Source: Israel Ministry of Foreign Affairs, "The Anti Terrorist Fence: Facts and Figures, February 2004." www.mfa.gov.

- Per capita income in Israel is over **$18,500,** putting it among the top 30 nations in the world. In 2005 its unemployment rate was **9 percent.**

- Per capita income among Palestinians in the Gaza and West Bank is less than **10 percent** that of Israelis. Palestinian unemployment has risen since 2000 to about **35 percent** overall and more than **50 percent** in Gaza.

Is Peace Possible in the Middle East?

❝Not only is vengeance against terrorism sometimes necessary, but it is more likely to bring peace if it is disproportionate. . . . True, terrorists may also argue that the way to alter Western policy is through violence. But that is all the more reason why the West must ensure its own victory first.❞

—Michael Rubin, *National Review Online.*

❝As long as American foreign policy remains the same and the Palestinian issue is left unresolved, the U.S. 'war on terror' will increase terrorism by 100 percent.❞

—Lebanese Shiite Muslim leader Grand Ayatollah Mohammed Hussein Fadlallah, 2004.

The question of peace in the Middle East is no longer just a matter of settling disputes between Israel and its neighbors. That long-running conflict is complex enough, but matters have become vastly more complicated by the U.S.-led invasion of Iraq. There, according to most analysts, a multiparty civil war has broken out. Furthermore, chaos in Iraq has allowed its powerful neighbor to the east, Iran, to become increasingly assertive in the Middle East. This has raised the specter of a regional conflict between Sunni Arab states such as Saudi Arabia and the Persian Shiite nation of Iran, or worse yet a nuclear conflict between Iran and Israel. At stake are not only the lives and fortunes of some 300 million people living in the Middle East but also the lion's share of the world's oil supply. Western powers have struggled to find their footing in this slippery Mideast situation. Nevertheless, a variety of peacemaking efforts are going forward.

Pull Out or Stay the Course?

Since 2001 the United States has sought to bring peace to the Middle East by military intervention, first in Afghanistan and subsequently in Iraq. Members of the Bush administration expressed confidence that by imposing democracy in those countries, America could set off a wave of democratization across the region that would lead to peace.

In particular, Bush administration officials testified before Congress that if America used military force to oust Iraq's dictator, people throughout the region would greet the invaders as liberators and embrace democracy. However, the strategy did not produce the desired results.

After a relatively easy victory in Iraq, the nation encountered new problems. Looting and chaos beset the country, followed by a violent insurgency against the occupying troops. Al Qaeda, which had little role in Iraq prior to the invasion, took advantage of the power vacuum to set up terrorist operations there. It drove the United Nations out of Iraq with two deadly bombings. It kidnapped foreign civilians, sometimes beheading them and posting videotape of their murders on the Internet. Above all, however, it fomented sectarian war between Shiites and Sunnis. This grim strategy proved all too effective.

> **After a relatively easy victory in Iraq, problems set in. Looting and chaos beset the country, followed by a violent insurgency.**

By 2007 no one called Iraq a beacon for Middle East democracy. Even the administration that once touted it as a democratic domino in the region shifted its position. In February 2007 the White House defended its Iraq strategy in negative terms: failure in Iraq, President George W. Bush said, would mean failure in the "War on Terror." He announced a new strategy involving a "surge" of U.S. troops intended to root out terrorists and militias.

Although democracy was achieved in Iraq, the daily violence, including almost incessant terrorist bombings, and the economic malaise caused thousands of the country's most talented people to flee, while those who remained became increasingly caught up in what most analysts termed a civil war.

In 2007 the White House and Congress came into open conflict over whether U.S. troops should remain in Iraq. Although Iraqi voters have approved a democratic constitution and elected a government, by all major measures of quality of life, Iraq is in decline. In the chaos that followed the collapse of Iraq's government al Qaeda wasted no time in setting up terrorist operations there. The terrorists hit on a strategy of pitting Shiites against Sunnis. Bombings of mosques and assassinations of clerics accomplished this goal, and at present daily sectarian massacres are a tragic feature of life in Iraq. An average of 100 Iraqi civilians die in bombings and killings every day. Many analysts, including some in the Pentagon, call it civil war.

The cost of U.S. involvement in Iraq has run to more than $400 billion, a total that continues to rise by more than $2 billion a week. The human toll is felt more keenly. Over 3,000 American troops and 800 American contractors have died in Iraq. Approximately 10 times that number have been wounded.

Bush continued to argue that defeating terrorists in Iraq was crucial to American security. He said America must stay until the democratically elected Iraqi government could defend itself. The Democratic-led Congress, however, disagreed. Democrats called for a "phased redeployment of U.S. forces,"[12] while calling on Iraq to shoulder responsibility for its security. A few Republicans agreed.

Dim Prospects for Iraqi Peace

Whether either course would produce peace in Iraq has been questioned. Citing numerous experts, *Newsweek* magazine asserted that a rapid pullout of U.S. troops would result in a flood of refugees heading across Iraq's borders and potentially destabilizing its neighbors. Iraq itself, already experiencing daily waves of violence, could plunge into a bloodbath, officials warned.

On the other hand, the Bush administration's last-ditch attempt to impose peace by force showed few signs of success by the spring of 2007. American troops sustained their highest casualties of the war over the six months from October 2006 through March 2007. In that period more than 500 U.S. soldiers died, about one-sixth of the total for the entire war.

Despite an all-out effort to secure the capital, bombings, after a brief lull, resumed with deadly effect. In April, for the first time, a suicide bomber penetrated the so-called Green Zone, a heavily fortified area where the Iraqi government and U.S. officials had enjoyed relative tranquillity. The bomb went off in the Iraqi parliament, killing the bomber and one legislator.

As violence continues unabated, the prevailing view among intelligence agencies, Congress, and, according to polls, the American people is that civil war has already erupted in Iraq; and no outside force can quench it. Civil wars do eventually exhaust themselves, but they sometimes last for decades. Complicating the Iraq situation is that Iran and Syria are both strongly suspected of fueling the conflict. In sum, no one can predict when peace will come to Iraq.

Israel and the Palestinians

Advocates of peace negotiations argue that the place to start—or rather, resume—is in Israel. If the United States puts its power and prestige on the line, they argue, a breakthrough is possible. America's Arab allies, such as Jordan, Saudi Arabia, and Egypt, have been pressing for such a step. So too has former U.S. president Jimmy Carter, who in 1978 successfully brokered a peace treaty between Israel and Egypt.

> " Former U.S. president Jimmy Carter is pressing for a just peace based on a reversal of Israel's settlement policy, which he charges has imprisoned Palestinians in cells within their own lands. "

Carter is pressing for a just peace based on a reversal of Israel's settlement policy. Carter believes the policy has imprisoned Palestinians in cells within their own lands. Carter's mission comes in the wake of years of a moribund peace process. After several U.S.-supported attempts to broker peace between the two sides in the 1990s, the peace process has yielded little or no subsequent progress between Israel and the Palestinians.

To be sure, the United States, the United Nations, Russia, and the European Union, acting as "the Quartet," have proposed a "Road Map" to peace. It too involves a withdrawal of Israelis from settlements in the occupied Palestinian lands. Palestinians have accepted it, but Israel has raised objections. In the five years since the Road Map was proposed in 2002, virtually no Israeli-Palestinian negotiations have taken place. Instead, the Palestinians launched another intifada, or uprising, this time relying heavily on suicide bombings.

A Unilateral Peace

Israel, under the government of Prime Minister Ariel Sharon, embarked in 2003 on a policy of unilateral disengagement from the Palestinians. Even after Sharon's felling by a stroke, the policy continues. It has been controversial both within and outside of Israel. It entails building what it calls a security fence along borders determined by Israel to keep hostile Palestinians out, and dismantling Jewish settlements in outlying areas. The main focus of the pullout has been Gaza, a 30-mile strip of land along the northwest coast of Israel with a small border abutting Egypt. More than 1 million Palestinians are crowded into the Gaza Strip, separated from the main body of Palestinians who live 30 miles away in the West Bank. Sharon reversed policy and forcibly pulled Israeli settlers out of Gaza, sealing the border as they left. He then turned his attention eastward to the West Bank. Sharon's plan has been violently opposed within Israel. The settler movement sees it as a betrayal of the sacred commitment to occupy all of ancient Israel. Others, particularly on Israel's right, see it as leaving Israel more vulnerable to rocket attacks from Palestinian territory.

International opinions vary. In general the Israeli move to disengage and withdraw from internationally recognized Palestinian lands has drawn applause. Bush in particular has endorsed the plan. However, the security fence that Israel is building along and through the West Bank has drawn vociferous objections from Palestinians and much international condemnation. The International Court of Justice ruled it illegal in 2004. The critics' chief complaint is that the "fence" is more of a wall that is being deliberately routed through Palestinian lands rather than along Israel's legitimate border. They note, moreover, that no substantial settlements in the West Bank have been dismantled. On the contrary, a system of Israeli-only highways continues to slice Palestinian lands into fragments in order to service Jewish settlements.

It is not clear whether a withdrawal from the West Bank is politically feasible in an Israel closely divided between pragmatists who see a defensible border as the chief goal and idealists who see occupation of the biblical lands of Judea and Samaria as a religious duty. All the same, proponents of the plan say that unilateral disengagement is the only way for Israel to settle issues with a fractious enemy that does not really want peace.

> " The critics' chief complaint is that the 'fence' is more of a wall that is being deliberately routed through Palestinian lands. "

Are Two States Viable?

Even if Israel were to withdraw from the West Bank as well as Gaza, questions remain about whether a Palestinian state would be viable. Critics point out that the Gaza Strip, which is home to more than a million Palestinians, is separated from the larger West Bank territory by a minimum of 34 miles of Israeli territory. Christian Aid states that 42 percent of the West Bank land is taken up by settlements and the infrastructure that supports them. In the land that remains under Palestinian control, economic resources are scant. This leads many analysts to doubt that a Palestinian state can survive on its own. Others, however, recall that in the early days of relative peace following the 1993 Oslo Accords, many Palestinians found work in Israel, and many Israelis shopped in Palestinian stores. An integrated two-state solution, therefore, might be viable. That, of course, would require an end to the mutual hatred and violence that has marked relations between the two peoples.

Clash of Civilizations

With the Israeli-Palestinian peace process stalled, the 9/11 attacks, and U.S. troops struggling to cope with a tide of violence in Iraq, some observers fear that a much larger conflict is taking shape. Historian Samuel P. Huntington is the leading exponent of this view. He describes the rising hostility between the West and Islam as a "clash of civilizations."[13] Huntington fundamentally disagrees with the key belief of neoconservatives, including Bush administration advisers who championed the invasion of Iraq, that people everywhere yearn for democracy. Those who accept Huntington's thesis believe that the entire Islamic world, which extends to Indonesia, Pakistan, Nigeria, and other places outside the Middle East, feels its values and way of life are under assault by the West. They believe that the Islamic world is waging a war of terror against the West, either to drive it out of Islamic lands, or, in the eyes of some, to establish the global supremacy of Islam.

There is evidence to suggest that, for some Muslims at least, this is true. While the vast majority of Muslims may be peaceful, there are currently Islamists (that is, Muslim extremists) who act out their grievances violently in every region of the world. This has been termed the globalization of terror. To name a few examples, in the 1990s Islamists attacked the Israeli embassy and friendship center in Argentina. In 1998 two U.S. embassies in East Africa were devastated by Islamist suicide bombers. In 2002 Islamist suicide bombers attacked the tourist district of Bali, a lovely Pacific island belonging to Indonesia. Hundreds were killed. Three years later, bombers struck there again. Other Islamic suicide bombers have caused devastation on commuter trains in Spain and subways and buses in London, England. On July 4, 2002, an Islamist gunman attacked the El Al airline ticket counter at Los Angeles International Airport. In India terrorists recently attacked the country's parliament, financial district, and the so-called peace train to Pakistan, while in Russia Chechen Muslim separatists have mounted numerous terrorist attacks, including a horrific 2004 assault on a rural Russian school in Beslan that ended in the deaths of nearly 400 children, teachers, and attackers.

No knowledgeable analyst suggests that all these attacks are coordinated, but they reflect widespread Muslim discontent with Western influence. To end this clash of civilization, clash-of-civilization theorists argue, will require generations of grinding conflict. Bush himself, who led the attack on Iraq in hope of democratizing the Middle East, appears to subscribe to this view. He has repeatedly said that the battle began on his watch, but will end during some other president's term.

Peace Now?

Conflict is indeed rife throughout the Middle East, and much of it involves shadowy groups whose suicidal tactics make them extremely difficult to deter, let alone defeat. Moreover, by every estimate the ranks of terrorist groups have grown since the U.S. invaded Iraq in 2003. A further threat to peace comes from Iran, which is developing nuclear capabilities in defiance of the United Nations. Nevertheless, this does not mean that the cause of peace is lost.

Governmental and nongovernmental efforts to end conflict in the Middle East continue. In 2002 Saudi Arabia initiated an Arab peace proposal, a new step for a nation long opposed to Israel. In 2007 that proposal was reaffirmed by the 22-nation Arab League. At about the same time, the Quartet—comprising the United States, European Union, Russia, and the United Nations—resolved to restart the "Roadmap" to peace effort. In March 2007 King Abdullah of Jordan flew to Washington to urge the United States to put its shoulder to the wheel. The European Community has also undertaken its own peace initiative.

> " In 2002 Saudi Arabia initiated an Arab peace proposal, a new step for a nation long opposed to Israel. "

Among the notable nongovernmental efforts are the model peace plan called the Geneva Accords and, more recently, an interfaith initiative of Christians, Muslims, and Jews to promote peace. On December 12, 2006, dozens of religious leaders from the three faiths signed a declaration calling on the United States to make Middle East peace a top priority.

There can be no doubt that the majority of people in all Middle Eastern countries want peace. Wherever polls are taken, this proves to be the case. Whether the peacemaking efforts can succeed, however, remains in question. Fanatics on all sides have shown the ability to derail peace on numerous occasions, and so many different interests are at work in the Middle East that satisfying everyone to the point of accepting compromise may not be possible. However, the alternative—increasingly vicious and pitiless conflict that destroys innocent lives, coarsens culture, and saps the wealth of nations—is even more unacceptable to most people. Therefore, it is certain that however slender the chances of success, the search for peace will continue.

Primary Source Quotes*

Is Peace Possible in the Middle East?

66 **What we did in Iraq in taking down Saddam Hussein was exactly the right thing to do. The world is much safer today because of it.** 99

—Dick Cheney, quoted in CNN.com, "Cheney: Talk of Blunders in Iraq Is 'Hogwash,'" January 27, 2007. http://i.a.cnn.net.

Cheney served as vice president of the United States in both terms of the George W. Bush administration.

66 **I am opposed to the escalation of American involvement in Iraq, including more U.S. troops. This is a danger- ously wrong-headed strategy that will drive America deeper into an unwinnable swamp at a great cost. It is wrong to place American troops into the middle of Iraq's civil war.** 99

—Chuck Hagel, "Hagel Statement on President Bush's Plan to Increase U.S. Troops in Iraq," U.S. Senator Chuck Hagel Press Office, January 10, 2007. http://hagel.senate.gov.

Hagel is a Republican U.S. senator from Nebraska and a decorated Army veteran.

Bracketed quotes indicate conflicting positions.

* Editor's Note: While the definition of a primary source can be narrowly or broadly defined, for the purposes of Compact Research, a primary source consists of: 1) results of original research presented by an organization or researcher; 2) eyewitness accounts of events, personal experience, or work experience; 3) first-person editorials offering pundits' opinions; 4) government officials presenting political plans and/or policies; 5) representatives of organizations presenting testimony or policy.

Primary Source Quotes

❝As long as Israel exists, the threat exists. As long as there is aggression against an Arab country, and as long as there is a war close to our borders, the danger continues. . . . Worry does not mean fear, but readiness for the confrontation.❞

—Bashar Al-Assad, interview by Talal Salman, *Al-Safir,* March 27, 2003. www.memri.org.

Assad is president of Syria.

❝Hezbollah will maintain its rocket arsenal as long as Iran continues its violent opposition to Israel's right to exist, the Assad regime retains control in Syria, and Hezbollah continues to leverage its militia for political power inside Lebanon.❞

—Patrick Devenny, "Hezbollah's Strategic Threat to Israel," *Middle East Quarterly,* Winter 2006. www.meforum.org.

Devenny is the Henry M. Jackson National Security Fellow at the Center for Security Policy in Washington, D.C.

❝In the Islamic world there is a natural tendency to resist the influence of the West, which is understandable given the long history of conflict between Islam and Western civilization. Obviously, there are groups in most Muslim societies that are in favor of democracy and human rights, and I think we should support those groups. But we then get into this paradoxical situation: many of the groups arguing against repression in those societies are fundamentalists and anti-American.❞

—Samuel P. Huntington, "So, Are Civilisations at War?" *Observer,* October 21, 2001. http://observer.guardian.co.uk.

Huntington is a professor of political science at Harvard University and author of the "clash of civilizations" view of Islam and the West.

---

66 The bottom line is this: Peace will come to Israel and the Middle East only when the Israeli government is willing to comply with international law, with the Roadmap for Peace, with official American policy, with the wishes of a majority of its own citizens—and honors its own previous commitments—by accepting its legal borders. **99**

—Jimmy Carter, *Palestine: Peace Not Apartheid.* New York: Simon & Schuster, 2006.

Carter was the thirty-ninth president of the United States. He won the 2002 Nobel Peace Prize for his peacemaking efforts in the Middle East.

66 This enemy is smart, capable, and unpredictable. They have defined a war on the United States, and I believe we're at war. I believe the attack on America made it clear that we're at war. I wish that wasn't the case. **99**

—George W. Bush, "President Bush Discusses the Global War on Terror in Tipp City, Ohio," Office of the Press Secretary, April 19, 2007. www.whitehouse.gov.

Bush is the forty-third president of the United States.

66 We must work together to restore Palestine, a nation in despair and without hope. We must work together to restore peace, hope and opportunity to the Palestinian people. And in so doing, we will begin a process of building peace, not only throughout the region, but throughout the world. **99**

—Abdullah II, "Address by His Majesty King Abdullah II," March 7, 2007. www.jordanembassyus.org.

Abdullah II is the king of Jordan.

66 The fence is solely a defensive measure, intended to protect Israelis from suicide bombings and other terrorist attacks. It is not a political act. It is not intended to be a border or to prejudge any future negotiations with the Palestinians. **99**

—Silvan Shalom, "Statement by Foreign Minister Silvan Shalom," March 17, 2004. http://securityfence.mfa.gov.il.

Shalom was Israel's foreign minister at the time he issued this statement in 2004.

66 Israel is under an obligation to terminate its breaches of international law; it is under an obligation to cease forthwith the works of construction of the wall being built in the Occupied Palestinian Territory, including in and around East Jerusalem, to dismantle forthwith the structure therein. **99**

—International Court of Justice, "Advisory Opinion: Legal Consequences of the Construction of a Wall in the Occupied Palestinian Territory," July 9, 2004. www.icj-cij.org.

The International Court of Justice is the principal judicial organ of the United Nations.

66 Both Islamists and secular Palestinians have come to see suicide bombing as a weapon against which Israel has no comprehensive defense. . . . Against the Palestinian H-bomb, Israel can at best build a fence. **99**

—Gal Luft, "The Palestinian H-Bomb: Terror's Winning Strategy," *Foreign Affairs,* July/August 2002. www.foreignaffairs.org.

Luft is an analyst and a former lieutenant colonel in the Israel Defense Force.

66 No Israeli government has ever tried to make peace on the formula that everybody knows is a winner: *Give back the land.* I don't mean give back the land except for the settlements, or the roads, or the military bases. I mean give back the land—the West Bank and Gaza. 99

—Richard Ben Cramer, *How Israel Lost: The Four Questions.* New York: Simon and Schuster, 2004.

Cramer won the 1979 Pulitzer prize for his Middle East reporting.

66 We have to put an end to this idea that if we give up our homes we will get something peaceful from terrorists. 99

—Yishai Hollender, quoted in Jennifer Medina, "Settlers' Defiance Reflects Postwar Israeli Changes," *New York Times,* April 22, 2007. www.nytimes.com.

Hollender is a spokesman for the Yesha Council, which represents Jewish settlers in the West Bank.

66 Under current conditions, a Palestinian state would be a terrorist state, bringing more war and terrorism. After all, sovereignty does not make a population and its leaders peaceful. Iran, North Korea and Syria are all sovereign states—are they peaceful and lovely? 99

—Morton A. Klein, "A Palestinian State Is Not the Answer," *Jewish Press,* February 7, 2007. www.zoa.org.

Klein is the president of the Zionist Organization of America.

66 We're being shelled and bombed and assassinated and killed. Our homes are being destroyed, our children traumatized. Our livelihoods, our institutions, our infrastructure totally demolished. 99

—Hanan Ashrawi, quoted in CNN.com, "13 Israeli Soldiers Killed in Apparent Ambush," April 9, 2002. http://archives.cnn.com.

Ashrawi is a Palestinian legislator and peace advocate.

Facts and Illustrations

Is Peace Possible in the Middle East?

- Iraq's first freely elected government gained recognition from the **United Nations Security Council** in June 2004. However, the government struggled to mount an effective police force in the face of a violent insurgency.

- As of April 2007 the U.S. Department of Defense had confirmed more than **3,300 U.S. service deaths** in Iraq since the 2003 invasion.

- **In spring 2007** Egypt agreed to host a conference of countries with an interest in Iraq to discuss how to bring peace to the troubled land.

- The Arab League, meeting in Saudi Arabia in 2007, endorsed for the second time a plan that offered Israel recognition and permanent peace with all Arab countries in return for Israeli withdrawal from lands captured in the **1967 Middle East** war and the creation of a Palestinian state.

- A December 2006 poll shows that **62 percent** of Palestinians and **68 percent** of Israelis support a compromise that would permanently end their conflict.

- A poll commissioned in **March 2007** by the Zionist Organization of America found that Americans opposed pressuring Israel to concede land to Palestinians.

U.S. Soldiers Continue to Die in Iraq

The death toll of U.S. forces stationed in Iraq has steadily mounted since the 2003 invasion. Various efforts to protect them, such as providing additional armor for vehicles and promotion of Iraqi defense forces, have not stemmed the rise in fatalities. By mid-2007, the cumulative toll was more than 3,400 U.S. service deaths.

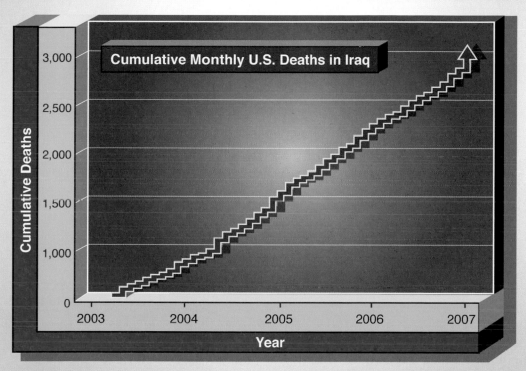

Source: Political Arithmetik, "Cumulative U.S. Deaths in Iraq," December 31, 2006. http://politicalarithmetik.blogspot.com.

- The **Hamas-led government** of the Palestinians has been unwilling to make a clear statement of acceptance of Israel's right to exist.

- **Israel's security barrier** has been ruled illegal by the International Court of Justice but has been approved by Israel's Supreme Court.

Civil War in Iraq Increases Turmoil and Suffering

Divisions between Sunnis and Shiites in Iraq have turned into a civil war that threaten regional stability as well as U.S. forces stationed there. Many families are leaving mixed areas for areas dominated by their own religious or ethnic group.

Displaced Families and Ethnic-Religious Areas in Iraq

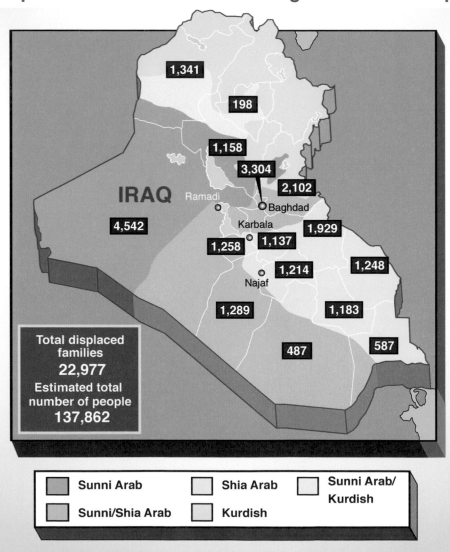

Source: BBC, "Iraq Violence: Facts and Figures," November 29, 2006. http://news.bbc.co.uk.

Extremists Find Support Among Minority of Muslims

Support for Muslim extremists is a minority position in virtually every Muslim community. Nevertheless, there is substantial support in many countries, amounting, experts say, to hundreds of millions of al Qaeda backers worldwide.

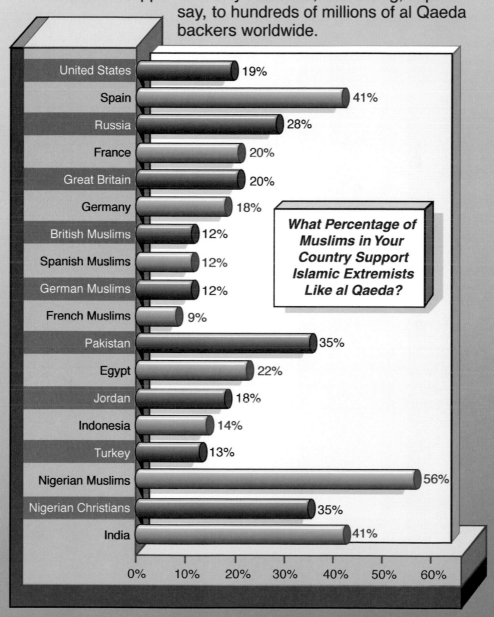

What Percentage of Muslims in Your Country Support Islamic Extremists Like al Qaeda?

Country	Percentage
United States	19%
Spain	41%
Russia	28%
France	20%
Great Britain	20%
Germany	18%
British Muslims	12%
Spanish Muslims	12%
German Muslims	12%
French Muslims	9%
Pakistan	35%
Egypt	22%
Jordan	18%
Indonesia	14%
Turkey	13%
Nigerian Muslims	56%
Nigerian Christians	35%
India	41%

Source: Pew Global Attitudes Project, "The Great Divide: How Westerners and Muslims View Each Other," June 12, 2006. http://pewglobal.org.

89

A Web of Interconnected Conflicts Bedevils the Middle East

Contemporary conflicts in the Middle East range far beyond the Israeli-Palestinian disputes. Nevertheless, many experts believe that finding an acceptable solution to those disputes is the first step to building a regional peace. The map below illustrates other major conflicts between religious groups in the Middle East.

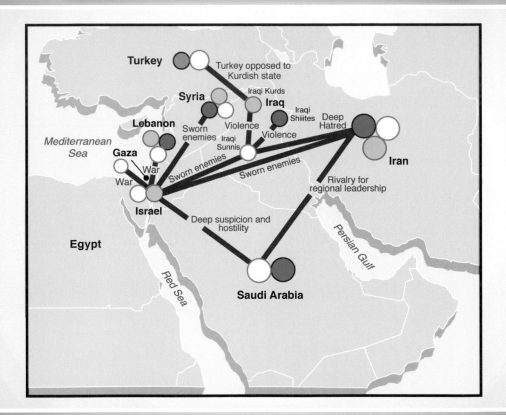

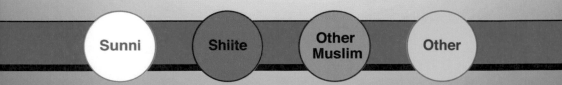

Source: Marc D. Charney, "Strife and Power in the New Middle East," New York Times, July 23, 2006. www.nytimes.com.

Key People and Advocacy Groups

Mahmoud Abbas: The president of the Palestinian National Authority, Abbas has attempted to be the voice of moderation but has been hampered by the majority party in the Palestinian government. Abbas represents the Fatah party, but the Islamist Hamas party holds a majority. In 2007 a national unity government split, with Abbas and his Fatah faction in armed conflict with Hamas, which controls Gaza.

King Abdullah II: The American-educated king of Jordan (his mother is American-born), Abdullah has been active in promoting a comprehensive regional peace beginning with settlement of the Palestinian-Israeli conflict.

Mahmoud Ahmadinejad: As president of Iran since 2005, Ahmadinejad has alarmed many in the West with his extremist rhetoric and advocacy of a nuclear development program in his country. Ahmadinejad has said that Israel should be "wiped off the map" (though some question the accuracy of this translation), and has rejected United Nations resolutions calling on Iran to halt its nuclear program.

AIPAC: The American Israel Public Affairs Committee is the leading pro-Israel lobby in Washington. Critics say it has excessive influence over U.S. policy in the Middle East; defenders say it promotes mutual interests of naturally friendly allies.

Yasir Arafat (1929–2004): Longtime chairman of the Palestine Liberation Organization and later president of its successor the Palestinian National Authority, Arafat was until his death the controversial emblem of his people. Reviled as a terrorist by some, he was a hero to many Palestinians.

Menachem Begin: Leader of a Zionist terrorist group during Israel's fight for independence, Begin later became a peacemaker. As prime minister of Israel he reached a historic peace settlement in 1978 with Egypt's president Anwar Sadat.

Osama bin Laden: Scion of a wealthy Saudi family, Bin Laden became radicalized by the Soviet invasion of Afghanistan. To help the Islamic underground resistance, he founded and led an organization called al Qaeda ("The Base"). After the Soviets withdrew, Bin Laden redirected al Qaeda's efforts toward driving Westerners—especially Americans—out of the Middle East. Following the 9/11 attacks on America, he has been in hiding but continues to release statements from time to time.

Gush Emunim: Hebrew for "Bloc of the Faithful," the organization worked from the mid-1970s on to rally support for Jewish settlement throughout the lands its members believed were granted them by God.

Theodore Herzl (1860–1904): Founder of modern Zionism, Herzl's calls for the establishment of a Jewish state in Palestine gained the loyalty of many European Jews, who envisioned a Jewish Socialist paradise away from a hostile Europe.

Saddam Hussein (1937–2006): Longtime dictatorial president of Iraq, Hussein became a notorious figure in the Middle East until his overthrow in 2003 by U.S.-led forces. Hussein launched unprovoked wars on two neighbors—Iran and Kuwait—and oversaw the commission of widespread atrocities against Shiites and Kurds in his country. He was executed on December 30, 2006.

Tzipi Livni: One of few women to reach the top ranks of Israeli leadership, Livni is the foreign minister of Israel. A protégé of Ariel Sharon, she is considered a step or two away from being prime minister.

Nouri al-Maliki: Maliki became prime minister of Iraq in April 2006 when competing factions could not agree on another candidate. A Shiite, he vowed to crack down on violence from all quarters, but his government proved ineffective and, critics said, far from impartial. The Interior Ministry was widely reported to be in the hands of militant Shiites, who used the police and prison system to persecute Sunnis.

Binyamin Netanyahu: Formerly the prime minister of Israel, Netanyahu leads the opposition in Israel. As prime minister from 1996 to 1999, he took a go-slow approach to implementing peace accords with the Palestinians and continues to promote a hard line.

Palestine Liberation Organization (PLO): From 1964 until 1993 the PLO was dedicated to the destruction of Israel. In the 1970s it became the world's most notorious terrorist organization for committing bloody hijackings and an assault on the 1972 Olympics. In 1993 it signed an agreement with Israel, known as the Oslo Accords, that were supposed to lay a path to peace. The accords were only partially implemented, and attacks on Israelis by PLO factions continued.

Peace Now: A liberal Israeli group, Peace Now has pressed for a peace agreement with Palestinians based on withdrawal from occupied territories and mutual recognition of statehood.

Anwar Sadat (1918–1981): Sadat rose through Egypt's army to become president of his country in 1970. Sadat led his nation to its most valiant yet ultimately futile war against Israel in 1973, and then four years later made a historic peace overture in an official visit to address Israel's parliament. The Camp David negotiation with Israeli prime minister Begin a year later resulted in a permanent peace treaty.

Moqtada al-Sadr: Militant leader of a major Shiite faction in Iraq, Sadr is the only surviving son of a famous Iraqi Shiite cleric who was assassinated by the regime of Saddam Hussein. His followers have formed a powerful militia known as the Mahdi Army. Sadr is believed to have close ties to Iran, where he was reported to be hiding out following an American-led crackdown on militia violence in 2007. However, Sadr's influence continues to be felt throughout Shiite strongholds in Iraq.

Ariel Sharon: A decorated general in the Israeli army, Sharon went on to a successful career in Israeli politics. Always a controversial figure, Sharon attracted widespread condemnation for allowing a massacre of unarmed Palestinians during Israel's 1982 invasion of Lebanon. After becoming prime minister in 2001, Sharon maintained a tough stance on Palestinians but surprised many with a unilateral withdrawal policy that he initiated in 2004. Following an incapacitating stroke in 2006, Sharon was removed from office.

Chronology

1916
Under the Sykes-Picot agreement, France and Britain agree to carve up the Ottoman Empire into colonial states. The resulting boundaries sow seeds of future conflicts both within and between Middle Eastern countries.

1979
Shiite clerics in Iran depose the U.S.-backed shah and declare an Islamic Republic. Revolutionary students, backed by the new Islamist government, seize the U.S. embassy and hold its staff hostage.

1095–1291
With the blessing of the pope and the Eastern Orthodox patriarch, European armies repeatedly assault the Islamic empire in hope of recapturing Jerusalem and the "Holy Land" for Christianity.

1948
David Ben-Gurion and his followers declare independence for Israel. War with Arab states immediately follows. In the chaos of war, hundreds of thousands of Palestinians are driven into exile.

1972
Palestinian terrorism captures the world's attention as the Black September faction seizes and murders Israeli athletes at the Munich Olympics.

1200 **1940** **1950** **1960** **1970**

1896
Theodor Herzl, the founding father of the Zionist movement, publishes his vision of a Jewish state in the Middle East.

1978
Egypt and Israel work out a permanent peace at Camp David in talks brokered by President Jimmy Carter.

1947
In the aftermath of World War II, the newly formed general assembly of the United Nations votes to partition Palestine into Jewish- and Arab-governed regions. Arab nations indignantly reject the plan.

1973
In a surprise attack on the Jewish holiday of Yom Kippur, Egyptian and Syrian forces score major successes. After the first assault, Israeli forces retake their lost ground and more, but the initial victory restores Egypt's sense of pride and opens a path to peace.

1967
Led by Egypt, Arab armies move toward Israel. In a preemptive strike, Israeli forces hurl themselves at Egypt, Jordan, and Syria, and in just six days capture Sinai and the Gaza Strip, the West Bank, and the Golan Heights. The United Nations Security Council passes Resolution 242, demanding that Israel withdraw from the conquered territories in return for lasting peace.

1980
Iraqi dictator Saddam Hussein, with the tacit support of the United States, launches a bloody eight-year war against neighboring Iran.

1993
Secret peace talks in Oslo, Norway, between Israel and the PLO lead to a preliminary peace deal, sealed by Palestinian leader Yasir Arafat and Israeli prime minister Yitzhak Rabin.

2003
The United States leads a narrow coalition of forces into Iraq to overthrow the regime of Hussein on the grounds that the dictator is stockpiling weapons of mass destruction. After a relatively easy conquest, it turns out that there are no such weapons to be found.

1990
Iraq invades Kuwait, taking over its oil fields. Hussein threatens that Saudi Arabia will be next.

1995
Yitzhak Rabin is assassinated by a young right-wing Jewish fanatic named Yigal Amir. The assassination, together with Palestinian suicide bombings in Israel, derails further progress on peace with the Palestinians.

1985   1990   1995   2000   2005

2001
The 9/11 suicide attacks on New York and Washington bring about a revolution in U.S. policy. Declaring war on terrorism, President George W. Bush adopts a policy of preventive use of force. It begins with an invasion of Afghanistan.

1987
Restive Palestinian youth launch the first intifada, or uprising, in the occupied territories.

2007
Iran, defying United Nations demands that it halt its nuclear program, declares that it has industrial scale uranium enrichment capabilities.

1991
A broad, U.S.-led coalition of forces drives Iraqi forces out of Kuwait in what comes to be known as Operation Desert Storm. President George H.W. Bush decides to halt the operation short of deposing Hussein.

2006
Hizballah launches rockets from Lebanon into Israel, including new longer-range rockets that strike some cities. Israel responds with a month-long military assault that devastates much of Lebanon.

Related Organizations

American-Arab Anti-Discrimination Committee

1732 Wisconsin Ave. NW

Washington, DC 20007

phone: (202) 244-2990

fax: (202) 244-7968

e-mail: president@adc.org

Web site: www.adc.org

Founded in 1980 by U.S. senator Jim Abourezk, the American-Arab Anti-Discrimination Committee (ADC) is a grassroots civil rights organization. Among its activities is the promotion of what it sees as a more balanced Middle East policy.

American Israel Public Affairs Committee

440 1st St. NW

Washington, DC, 20001

phone: (202) 639-5200

Web site: www.aipac.org

The American Israel Public Affairs Committee (AIPAC) works to make Israel more secure by ensuring that American support remains strong. It has more than 100,000 members and enjoys regular access to the top U.S. leadership in Washington, D.C. Among its current goals are to stop Iran's nuclear program, which many fear may be aimed at developing nuclear weapons.

Council for the National Interest

1250 4th St. SW

Suite WG-1

Washington, DC 20024

phone: (202) 863-2951

e-mail: inform@cnionline.org

Web site: www.cnionline.org

Founded by former Illinois congressman Paul Findley, the Council for the National Interest seeks to reorient U.S. foreign policy in the Middle East from what it sees as a one-sided, pro-Israel position to one that is more consistent with American national interests. In addition to a peace settlement in the Middle East, it seeks an end to unaudited U.S. aid to Israel.

Council on Foreign Relations

Harold Pratt House

58 E. 68th St.

New York, NY 10021

phone: (212) 434-9400

fax: (212) 434-9800

e-mail: communications@cfr.org

Web site: www.cfr.org

The Council on Foreign Relations is an independent, nonpartisan center for scholars dedicated to providing analysis and ideas to help its members, as well as policy makers, journalists, students, and interested citizens, to better understand the world and the foreign policy choices facing the United States and other governments.

Embassy of Israel

3514 International Dr. NW

Washington, DC 20008

phone: (202) 364-5542

fax: (202) 364-5423

e-mail: info@israelemb.org

Web site: www.israelemb.org

The embassy is Israel's official representative to the United States, headed by its ambassador to Washington. Its Web site includes up-to-date news about the peace process, as well as background materials. The embassy also maintains a speaker's bureau and educational materials.

Foundation for Middle East Peace

1761 N St. NW

Washington, DC 20036

phone: (202) 835-3650

fax: (202) 835-3651

e-mail: info@fmep.org

Web site: www.fmep.org

Established in 1979, the foundation is dedicated to promoting, through various activities, a just solution to the Israeli-Palestinian conflict that brings peace and security to both peoples. The foundation takes a critical view of Israeli settlements in the Occupied Territories.

Middle East Institute

1761 N St. NW

Washington, DC 20036

phone: (202) 785-1141

fax: (202) 331-8861

e-mail: mideasti@mideasti.org

Web site: www.mideasti.org

Since its founding in 1946 by a former secretary of state, the Middle East Institute has been an important conduit of information between Middle Eastern nations and American policy makers, organizations, and the public. It strives to increase knowledge of the Middle East among our own citizens and to promote understanding between the peoples of the Middle East and America.

Middle East Studies Association

1219 N. Santa Rita Ave.

University of Arizona

Tucson, AZ 85721

phone: (520) 621-5850

fax: (520) 626-9095

e-mail: mesana@u.arizona.edu

Web site: www.mesana.org

The Middle East Studies Association (MESA) is a private, nonprofit, non-political learned society that brings together scholars, educators, and those interested in the study of the region from all over the world. As part of its goal to advance learning, facilitate communication, and promote cooperation, MESA sponsors an annual meeting that is a leading international forum for scholarship and intellectual exchange about the Middle East.

Palestinian National Authority State Information Service

PO Box 5075

Gaza City

Gaza, Palestine

e-mail: info@sis.gov.ps

Web site: www.sis.gov.ps.

The State Information Service (SIS) is a Palestinian governmental institution affiliated with the Office of the President of the Palestinian National Authority. The SIS was founded by a presidential decree on February 12, 1996. Since then the SIS has been working as the official body responsible for organizing and developing information and media activities in the Palestinian-governed territories.

U.S. Department of State, Bureau of Near Eastern Affairs

2201 C St. NW

Washington, DC 20520

phone: (202) 647-4000

The State Department is the federal government's cabinet-level agency devoted to international relations, and the Near East Bureau focuses on Middle Eastern affairs. Concerning Middle East conflicts, the State Department's mission includes this statement: "The United States is committed to achieving the vision of two states, Israel and Palestine, living side-by-side in peace, security, and dignity. We seek to end terrorism and achieve a permanent reconciliation between the Israeli and Palestinian peoples. The United States, in consultation with the European Union, Russia, and the United Nations, and in partnership with the Israeli, Palestinian, and Arab governments, will work to promote a lasting peace."

Zionist Organization of America

4 East 34th St.

New York, NY 10016

phone: (212) 481-1500

fax: (212) 481-1515

e-mail: info@zoa.org

Web site: www.zoa.org

Founded in 1897, the Zionist Organization of America has a national membership of over 30,000 with chapters throughout the United States. The ZOA works to strengthen U.S.-Israeli relations through educational activities, public affairs programs, media and campus activities, and lobbying in Washington.

For Further Research

Books

Said K. Aburish, *Saddam Hussein: The Politics of Revenge.* London, Bloomsbury, 2001.

Antony Black, *The History of Islamic Political Thought: From the Prophet to the Present.* Edinburgh, Scotland: Edinburgh University Press, 2001.

David Cook, *Understanding Jihad.* Berkeley: University of California Press, 2005.

Alan Dershowitz, *The Case for Israel.* Hoboken, NJ: John Wiley & Sons, 2004.

Norman Finkelstein, *Image and Reality of the Israel-Palestine Conflict.* 2nd ed. New York: Verso, 2003.

Arthur Goldschmidt, *Concise History of the Middle East.* Boulder, CO: Westview, 2005.

Albert Hourani, *A History of the Arab Peoples.* Cambridge, MA: Harvard University Press, 1991.

R. Stephen Humphreys, *Between Memory and Desire: The Middle East in a Troubled Age.* Berkeley: University of California Press, 2001.

Mark Juergensmeyer, *Terror in the Mind of God: The Global Rise of Religious Violence.* 3rd ed. Berkeley: University of California Press, 2003.

Rashid Khalidi, *Resurrecting Empire: Western Footprints and America's Perilous Path in the Middle East.* Boston, MA: Beacon, 2005.

Bernard Lewis, *From Babel to Dragomans: Interpreting the Middle East.* New York: Oxford University Press, 2004.

——, *What Went Wrong?: The Clash Between Islam and Modernity in the Middle East.* New York: HarperCollins, 2003.

Sandra Mackey, *The Reckoning: Iraq and the Legacy of Saddam Hussein.* New York: W.W. Norton, 2002.

Ann Elizabeth Mayer, *Islam and Human Rights: Tradition and Politics.* Boulder, CO: Westview, 1998.

Vali Nasr, *The Shia Revival: How Conflicts Within Islam Will Shape the Future.* New York: W.W. Norton, 2006.

Michael B. Oren, *Power, Faith, and Fantasy: America in the Middle East: 1776 to the Present.* New York: W.W. Norton, 2007.

———, *Six Days of War: June 1967 and the Making of the Modern Middle East.* New York: Random House, 2003.

David Pryce-Jones, *The Closed Circle: An Interpretation of the Arabs.* Chicago: Irvin R. Dee, 2002.

Barry Rubin, *The Modern Middle East.* Cambridge: Cambridge University Press, 2002.

Charles D. Smith, *Palestine and the Arab-Israeli Conflict.* 5th ed. New York: Bedford/St. Martin's, 2004.

Periodicals

Agence France Press and Associated Press, "Iraqi Death Toll Estimates Go as High as 150,000," *Taipei Times*, November 11, 2006. www.taipeitimes.com.

Samar Assad, "The Palestinian Unity Government: An Opportunity for U.S. Diplomacy," *Jerusalem Media and Communication Centre*, March 15, 2007. www.jmcc.org.

Associated Press, "Annan: Life for Iraqis Worse than with Saddam," *MSNBC*, December 4, 2006. www.msnbc.msn.com.

Jeffrey Bartholet, "Sword of the Shia," *Newsweek*, December 4, 2006. www.msnbc.msn.com.

Brian Bennett, "Inside the Green Zone," *Time*, April 26, 2007. www.time.com.

Louis Rene Beres, "Israel's Uncertain Strategic Future," *Parameters*, Spring 2007. www.carlisle.army.mil.

Praful Bidwai, "Inside Iran Today," *International News*, April 27, 2007. www.thenews.com.

Richard Boudreaux, "Israel Sounds Alarm on Iran's Nuclear Efforts," *Los Angeles Times*, February 7, 2007. www.latimes.com.

Massimo Calabresi, "Iran's Nuclear Threat," *Time*, March 8, 2003. www.time.com.

Dan Eggen, "Bin Laden, Most Wanted for Embassy Bombings?" *Washington Post*, August 28, 2006. www.washingtonpost.com.

William Engdahl, "A New American Century?—Iraq and the Hidden Euro-Dollar Wars," *Current Concerns*, April 2003. www.currentconcerns.ch.

Jamie Glasov, "Boys of the Taliban," *FrontPage*, January 1, 2007. www.frontpagemag.com.

Conn Hallinan, "Iran and Beyond: Shi'ite vs. Sunni?" *ZNet*, April 24, 2007. www.zmag.org.

Alexander G. Higgins, "U.N.: 100,000 Iraq Refugees Flee Monthly," *Boston Globe*, November 3, 2006. www.boston.com.

Sarah E. Kreps, "The 2006 Lebanon War: Lessons Learned," *Parameters*, Spring 2007. www.carlisle.army.mil.

Ruth Lapidoth, "Legal Aspects of the Palestinian Refugee Question," *Jerusalem Letter*, September 2002. www.jcpa.org.

Dan Murphy, "How Al Qaeda Views a Long Iraq War," *Christian Science Monitor*, October 6, 2006. www.csmonitor.com.

Dion Nissenbaum, "Death Toll of Israeli Civilians Killed by Palestinians Hit a Low in 2006," McClatchy Newspapers, January 10, 2007. www.realcities.com.

Trita Parsi, "Europe's Mendacity Doomed Iran Talks to Failure," *Financial Times*, August 30, 2005. www.ft.com.

Walter Pincus, "Violence in Iraq Called Increasingly Complex," *Washington Post*, November 17, 2006. www.washingtonpost.com.

Uzi Rubin, "Hizballah's Rocket Campaign Against Northern Israel: A Preliminary Report," *Jerusalem Issue Brief*, August 31, 2006. www.jcpa.org.

Karen Ruster and Sammy Salama, "A Preemptive Attack on Iran's Nuclear Facilities: Possible Consequences," *Center for Nonproliferation Studies*, September 9, 2004. http://cns.miis.edu.

Ben Thein, "Is Israel's Security Barrier Unique?" *Middle East Quarterly*, Fall 2004. www.mcforum.org.

Web Sites

Afghanistan Online (www.afghan-web.com). Afghanistan Online is a privately owned, independent Web site that provides updated news and information on Afghanistan. The site has information on virtually all aspects of life and culture in Afghanistan, including its recent history under Taliban rule and the Western invasion that brought democracy to the country.

Al Jazeera (http://english.aljazeera.net). An independent news network based in Bahrain, Al Jazeera's English-language Web site presents news from and about the Middle East from an Arab perspective.

Americans for Peace Now (www.peacenow.org). An affiliate of the Israeli Shalom Achshav ("Peace Now") organization, Americans for Peace Now (APN) was founded in 1981. APN is the leading United States advocate for peace in the Middle East. Its Web site includes newsletters and publications.

Ha'aretz (www.haaretz.com). One of Israel's leading newspapers presents this online English-language version. It contains daily news about the Middle East from an Israeli perspective.

Hizballah (www.hizbollah.org). Hizballah is a Shiite militia and political organization in Lebanon. Its English-language site includes interviews with Hizballah leaders and statements of its positions on conflicts with Israel and the United States.

International Policy Institute for Counter-Terrorism (www.ict.org.il). The Israel-based International Policy Institute for Counter-Terrorism (ICT) is an independent think tank providing expertise in terrorism, counter-terrorism, homeland security, threat vulnerability and risk assessment, intelligence analysis, and national security and defense policy. Its Web site has a wealth of information and analysis on Islamic terrorism.

Israel Ministry of Foreign Affairs (www.mfa.gov.il/mfa). This official site of the government of Israel contains a wealth of information about the country's conflicts with its neighbors. Among them are sections on the threat from Iran, Israel's claim to all of Jerusalem as its capital, and the peace process with the Palestinians.

Middle East Network Information Center (http://menic.utexas.edu). The Middle East Network Information Center (MENIC) is a service of the University of Texas Center for Middle East Studies. The site contains summary information on many countries of the Middle East, as well as the arts and humanities, business and economy, and governments of the region.

Middle East Report (www.middleeast.org). A Washington-based online and print resource, this site offers views critical of Israel and U.S. policy toward the Middle East.

MidEast Web (www.mideastweb.org). This is a Web site created by peace activists from both sides of the Arab-Israeli conflict. It is a registered nongovernmental organization in Israel. The site contains up-to-date news and commentary about Middle East affairs.

Tikkun (www.tikkun.org). The site of a progressive Jewish organization, founded by Rabbi Michael Lerner, it contains articles of analysis on the Israeli-Palestinian conflict and American Jewish attitudes toward it.

Source Notes

How Has the Rise of Islamic Militancy Affected Middle East Conflicts?

1. Quoted in MEMRI, "Criticism of Tehran Holocaust Denial Conference in Arab and Iranian Media," Special Dispatch Series, no. 1425, January 16, 2007. www.spme.net.
2. Quoted in Reuters, "EU Views Iran Nuclear Statement with 'Great Concern,'" April 10, 2007. www.alertnet.org.

How Does U.S. Involvement Affect the Middle East?

3. Mitchell Bard, "U.S.-Israel Relations: A Special Alliance," Jewish Virtual Library, 2007. www.jewishvirtuallibrary.org.

How Does the Arab-Israeli Conflict Affect the Middle East?

4. David Horovitz, *Still Life with Bombers*. New York: Alfred A. Knopf, 2004. p. 22.
5. Quoted in Associated Press, "Palestinians Attack Jewish Settlement," *News Max.com Wires*, May 20, 2005. www.newsmax.com.
6. Christian Aid, "Facts on the Ground: The End of the Two State Solution?" October 2004, p. 7. www.christianaid.org.uk.

7. United Nations Security Council, "U.N. Security Council Resolution 242," November 22, 1967. www.mideastweb.org.
8. George W. Bush, "Letter to Prime Minister Sharon," April 14, 2004. www.fmep.org.
9. Quoted in National Public Radio, "Jimmy Carter Defends 'Peace Not Apartheid,'" January 25, 2007. www.npr.org.
10. U.S. Department of State, "Country Reports on Human Rights Practices—2006: Israel and the Occupied Territories," March 6, 2007. www.state.gov.
11. Richard Ben Cramer, *How Israel Lost*. New York: Simon & Schuster, 2004, p. 11.

Is Peace Possible in the Middle East?

12. Senate and House Democrats, "Real Security: Protecting America and Restoring Our Leadership in the World," March 29, 2006, p. 96. http://democrats.senate.gov.
13. Samuel P. Huntington, *The Clash of Civilizations and the Remaking of World Order*. New York: Simon & Schuster, 1996.

List of Illustrations

List of Illustrations

Index

About the Author

Clay Farris Naff is an award-winning journalist, nonprofit executive, and author. His wide international experience includes years of living and traveling in the Middle East. In the early 1990s, while a Tokyo-based correspondent for United Press International and National Public Radio, he reported on Japan's reluctant involvement in the first Gulf War. His first book, the 1994 nonfiction title *About Face: How I Stumbled onto Japan's Social Revolution*, brought him a National Endowment for the Humanities fellowship. Naff serves as executive director of the Lincoln Literacy Council in Lincoln, Nebraska.